D0867990

Praise for *Sacred Grief*

"A powerful exploration of a universal human experience! Using true-life accounts and personal examples, Leslee Tessmann masterfully leads us beyond the process of grief itself, into a bold new perspective of our lifelong relationship with change. Because we will all have the experience, *Sacred Grief* is a compelling guide for everyone searching for the sweetness in life's great passages."   —Gregg Braden, author
The Divine Matrix and *The God Code*

"With sensitivity and grace, Leslee Tessmann leads the reader through a dark and difficult passage into the light of awareness, acceptance, and new aliveness. *Sacred Grief* is a holy handbook for gleaning the gifts of the journey called grief."   —Mary Manin Morrissey
Co-Founder, Assn. for Global New Thought

"Many thanks to Leslee Tessmann for this significant contribution to our understanding of grief. *Sacred Grief* presents a perspective not only on the grieving process, but on how a fresh context for that process can transform the experience as whole. *Sacred Grief* is a welcome departure from the conventional advice about 'surviving' grief."
—Jill Carroll, Ph.D., Executive Director,
Boniuk Center for the Study and Advancement of
Religious Tolerance, Rice University

"I highly recommend this book to anyone that has experienced any type of loss in their lives and is willing to look at the loss through a different set of eyes. Tessman, in *Sacred Grief,* will lead the reader to a place of compassion for oneself , create a relationship with his/her own grief, and ultimately create a place of understanding and a healed soul."

—Irene Watson, Managing Editor,
Reader Views

"I enjoyed the book very much. Rather than the old strategy to try to suppress or manipulate one's way through life and grief, *Sacred Grief* provides readers with a new path, a new way of being in the world with their grief."

—Marc Levine, MA, MFCT, Bellevue, WA

"*Sacred Grief* was so honest and real, it just touched my heart. Leslee gives definitions and solutions that make complete sense, almost like we should know this information from a primal instinct but we don't until she shares her inspirational insights learned through her own pain and grief. It is a book I will read again and give to my friends and family."

—Tammye Read, Seattle, WA

"Sacred Grief makes sense. Unlike most of our culture's conversation about death and grieving, this book is not concerned with 'fixing' or 'getting rid' of grief. Instead, Leslee Tessmann creates a context for grief that is as practical as it is inspiring. As a young woman who recently experienced the sudden death of a parent, I know that there is no easy way through grief. But the opportunity to relate to our grief as sacred is the most powerful tool we can have during those times when we feel our most powerless."

—Nishta Mehra, Houston, TX

"In *Sacred Grief*, Leslee generously gives us an intimate look at her journey through an event most of will experience but few of us are willing to discuss, much less embrace. While there is no way to avoid pain and sadness after the death of a loved one, she shows us that suffering is optional when we approach grief with an attitude of acceptance and curiosity rather than fear and resistance. A good book to learn how to be gentle with yourself when life is feeling harsh."

—Beryl Kaminsky, LPC, CT
Grief Counselor, Houston, TX

"Leslee Tessmann tells her compelling personal story in a compassionate, strong voice. *Sacred Grief* offers gentle wisdom on a tough subject and provides a message the world needs to hear."

—Donna Walker, Librarian, Denver, CO

"This book gave me an unexpected view of grief—to actually cherish the moments of my grief without indulging in the emotions, and then move on. Leslee's generous sharing of her story allowed me to accept more of myself and carry that acceptance and the sacredness of every moment into all of my life."

—Linda Fraser, Houston, TX

LESLEE TESSMANN

SACRED GRIEF

Exploring a New
Dimension to Grief

Copyright (2008) Leslee Tessmann. All Rights Reserved.

No part of this publication may be reproduced, transmitted in any form or by any means, electronic, mechanical, photocopying, recording, or other otherwise, or stored in a retrieval system, without the prior written consent of the publisher.

First Edition: April 2008

Library of Congress Cataloging-in-Publication Data

Tessmann, Leslee, 1953-
  Sacred grief : exploring a new dimension to grief / Leslee Tessmann.
    p. cm.
  Includes bibliographical references and index.
  ISBN-13: 978-1-932690-53-8 (trade paper : alk. paper)
  ISBN-10: 1-932690-53-0 (trade paper : alk. paper)
  1. Grief. I. Title.
  BF575.G7T46 2008
  155.9'37--dc22

                                    2008002569

Published by:
Loving Healing Press
5145 Pontiac Trail
Ann Arbor, MI 48105
USA

http://www.LovingHealing.com or
info@LovingHealing.com
Fax +1 734 663 6861

Loving Healing Press

This book is lovingly dedicated to
my father and mother,
LeRoy and Jean Tessmann.

Thank you for inspiring me with your love,
courage, and respect for life.

Table of Contents

Acknowledgements

The manifestation of *Sacred Grief* is a community effort and victory. What began as a divine thought from the source of all life was lovingly guided through the lives and hearts of many. Perhaps every writer is faced with the dilemma of how to acknowledge all who have contributed to one's written work. It would be impossible to list everyone, just as it would be impossible not to acknowledge anyone. My desire is that everyone who has touched my life and helped inspire *Sacred Grief* accepts the following as an acknowledgment for themselves as well. I offer my heartfelt appreciation and gratitude for your contribution towards the fulfillment of this tender and creative work.

From the very beginning, I have been blessed by my mother, Jean Tessmann, and her steadfast faith and belief in my dream to write a book that would make a difference for others. Her ongoing prayers were generously offered and lovingly propelled me forward each step of the way. I could not have asked for a more loving, caring, and giving mother and friend.

The heart of *Sacred Grief* comes from the lessons I constantly learn from my siblings—Dolores, Mary, Jim, Carol and Allen, and my daughter, Jennifer, and grandchildren, Maxwell, Lexus, and Lydia Grace. They have all been the perfect teachers of one of life's greatest paradoxes—that the depth of love one experiences is entirely dependent on the willingness to open one's heart and accept another exactly as they are and as they are not. Thank you for the love you generously offer and the difference it made in the unfolding of *Sacred Grief.*

I offer deep gratitude and respect for Victor Volkman for his partnership in manifesting my first book and for his wisdom, courage, and the integrity he brought to the birthing and publishing of *Sacred Grief.*

This would be just another self-help book on the shelf were it not for Sandy Lawrence's brilliant promotional guidance and willingness to help hold the vision for *Sacred Grief's* contribution to each life touched by its message of freedom and peace.

I thank Irene Watson, my agent, for her loving and straightforward guidance in paving the way for *Sacred Grief* to be published by Loving Healing Press, and her willingness to explore and experience firsthand all that the book offered so that she might authentically express that in her reviews.

Editing one's book and labor of love is a delicate endeavor. Consequently, I owe great thanks and appreciation to Mark Bruni and Stephanie Gunning who were instrumental in using their extraordinary editing talents and skills to bring clarity to *Sacred Grief*'s powerful message.

I also offer deep appreciation and thanks to Gregg Braden, Mary Manin Morrissey, and Jill Carroll for their generous endorsement *of Sacred Grief* and for taking time from their immensely full lives and demanding schedules to read the manuscript and offer wisdom and encouragement along the way. It's difficult to stop or hold back when one is being called to be by such powerful and extraordinary human beings such as Gregg, Mary and Jill.

So many great friends offered their love, support, and wisdom to keep the vision for *Sacred Grief* alive and encouragement to keep going whenever I began to doubt or question myself: Linda Fraser, Trina Marquez, Tammye Read, Marc Levine, Ed and Joanne Schmidt, Anita McHarg, Amy Larsen, Lynn Boyd, Michelle Land, Deborah Enderle, Evelyn Heaton, Steve Braun, Marta Defex, Kim Reeves, Aileen Sanchez, Nan Stombaugh, Sarah Wyckoff, Liz Zalazar, and many others from my spiritual family at Unity

Church of Christianity in Houston, To all of you, I offer my love, appreciation, and gratitude.

A special heartfelt thanks needs to be expressed to Marjie Parrot for participating in my personal transformation and helping me remove the obstacles that held me back from following my heart and "singing my song". Marjie, I am eternally indebted to you for unlocking my passion, living my calling, and opening my heart to the world.

Last of all—and perhaps the one acknowledgment that touches my heart the deepest—is that of my father, LeRoy Tessmann. Dad, thank you for being such an amazing father and for teaching me about courage, commitment, and the power of faith and prayer. I love and miss you deeply. Wherever you are, the world is a better place because of your presence.

Preface

Sacred Grief is a book whose message and time have come. Up until now, human beings, particularly in the Western world, have turned to established theories about the grief process. Sigmund Freud's "tasks of grief" and Elisabeth Kübler-Ross' writings on the stages of grief have significantly expanded our capacity to overcome the more challenging losses in our lives. However, we live in such complicated times that the circumstances surrounding today's losses are no longer as simple as they once were. Consequently, we are challenged to go deeper and take a fresh look at what the grief process is all about.

Along with the "ordinary" although profound losses attributed to disease, suicide, drug and alcohol abuse, accidents, natural catastrophes, and divorce we are now dealing with aggressive cancers, white-collar crime such as the Enron scandal, gang violence, school shootings, and acts of terrorism. Grief associated with these types of losses is deep, long lasting, and complicated. Today's violent criminal acts have left a wake of children confronted with the loss of parents and siblings to traumatic and unimaginable circumstances. Global conflicts have surpassed the horrors of past wars: Viet Nam was a catastrophe and Iraq is a living nightmare. Add all of that to the "ordinary" events I mentioned above and we're left with a large part of humanity dealing with deep, complicated, and, most likely, unresolved grief.

So we now need to consider that our current understanding of the grief process is not enough to move us through the depth and complexity of these losses. In fact, it seems that we are being forced to give up understanding and just be with the pain, because with many of these circumstances there is no understanding. Mostly what there is, is pain. But human beings, especially in the Western world, resist pain and will do whatever they can to avoid it. Rather than work with the body's natural healing process, we search for answers and explanations in a desperate attempt to understand and strike back at that which took the life of our loved one. But there is a point at which we cross a fine line where the drive to understand becomes the means to either indulge in or suppress our pain.

Unfortunately, it isn't enough that we endure the natural suffering caused by life's unexpected turn of events. We're human beings with language, so we add to it by layering non-stop judgments of what we are experiencing on top of the suffering already there, which produces yet more judgment and an endless cycle of self-induced suffering. Grief becomes a dirty or bad word, or worse, the enemy. That's exactly how, up until now, we've related to it, and that's exactly why our suffering goes far beyond that which the natural process of grief would have us endure.

The choice to relate to grief this way may be unconscious, but nonetheless it is still a choice. The impact of that choice can be extensive: years of depression, complex emotional and physical health issues, and the acting out of anger, blame, guilt, self-pity, and sadness for a large portion of our lives. Our most cherished relationships and the fulfillment of our lives are drastically impaired, if not completely cut off. It doesn't have to be this way. In fact, I assert that the natural unfolding of our lives would have us say "No more!" Thus, *Sacred Grief*.

I lived a large portion of my life as I have just described. The circumstances may not have been as complicated as those we face today, but the result was the same—a tremendous amount of unnecessary, self-induced suffering, and a delay in the natural unfolding of life. Ever since discovering this, my journey has been about exploring what moved me along that path and my relationship to grief. *Sacred Grief* recounts that journey and invites readers to consider what might be possible if we were to consciously create a friendly, non-aggressive relationship to grief. A relationship whose context would be more than just a process; it would be sacred. As such, reverence and respect would be given to every loss, emotion, and moment of our grief.

The book takes readers through a discussion of what gets in the way of moving through one's grief with compassion and kindness. It doesn't assume to tell them how to create a friendly relationship to grief, but rather nudges them into the unfamiliar and uncertain, that fertile space of creation. Moving into that space allows the reader to shift their perception of grief, death, and loss such that they can work with grief on its terms—its duration, depth, and expression—with kindness and respect. From there, *Sacred Grief* opens the path to surrender, a surrendering that brings peace and allows one to experience grief with curiosity rather than disgust, and to embrace its unexpected, exquisite gifts.

There are thousands of books about grief. Many of them eloquently explain and explore the grief process, death and dying, pain, suffering, and grief's impact on family dynamics. But I have yet to discover a single book that addresses our relationship to grief and the quality of life available if we consciously relate to grief as sacred—one that poses the possibility of using language to powerfully shift our relationship to a process that is such a pervasive part of our everyday lives. *Sacred Grief* opens the door to that conversation.

This book stands on the shoulders of contemporary authors such as Thomas Moore, Elisabeth Kübler-Ross, Steven Levine, and Ram Dass. It also expands on Sigmund Freud's and other contemporary psychologists' observations and significant writings regarding the "tasks" of grief. In 1969, Kübler-Ross brilliantly laid the groundwork for defining, understanding, and working with the stages of death and grief. However, it's time to take that work a quantum leap further by taking a closer look at our relationship to grief. It's the missing piece that will allow us to declare "sacred" as the context to our grief, and ultimately to our lives.

The personal result of reading *Sacred Grief* is movement forward with one's life with peace, purpose, and passion, intimately aware of the sacredness and fragility of every given moment. The global result of *Sacred Grief* is an eternal well of compassion and a shift in mankind moving through years of unresolved grief. That ripple effect is massive and allows each and every human being to participate in the natural unfolding of our planet. Ultimately, if we allow grief to become our ally or friend, we might actually experience the world as our friend, no matter how it looks. For that to happen, we have to give up our expectations and agendas. The true essence of world peace lies in being with things just the way they are and it will require compassion on the part of everyone to experience the workability of the world, no matter how it looks, for longer than a few fleeting seconds. Our global existence therefore depends on compassion. *Sacred Grief* boldly asks, "Are you willing to join forces with your grief so that the world can experience itself as all that it can be?" That is a question whose time, like *Sacred Grief*, has also come.

Introduction

Going Beyond Survival:
Exploring a New Dimension to Grief

Well, here it is—another book on grief. I suspect that's one thought that may have crossed
your mind when your eye caught the title of this
book. The other thought you may have enter-
tained might have been something like, "Sacred?
That's interesting. I can't imagine relating to grief
as sacred." Finding that concept interesting indicates curiosity, and curiosity will make all the
difference as you read on and explore further.
Finding that concept unimaginable indicates no
prior reference point to what a sacred relationship to grief might look like. That space of "can't
imagine" is the perfect place from which to create
something new and unimaginable.

Unlike many of its predecessors, *Sacred Grief*
is not about the grief process. Rather, it is about
our relationship to grief. For most human beings,
we aren't aware that we have a relationship with

grief, so how we typically relate to it is unconscious and automatic. We move through the
process via knee-jerk reactions to a vast array of
emotions based on our opinions about what grief
should and shouldn't look like. Without realizing
it, these opinions become the essence, or context,
of our relationship to grief and have a tremendous impact on the quality of our lives and on
our experience of life. We will explore context at
greater length later on, but for now let's associate
it with essence.

Exploring one's relationship to grief interests
and excites me because my personal experience,
as well as my observations of others, indicates
that there is a fine line between understanding
the grief process and actually experiencing the
grief process. Somewhere on either side of this
line there is unnecessary, self-induced suffering—far more than the natural grief process already provides.

There are literally thousands of books about
the grief process, of which several have made a
tremendous difference in dealing with my own
grief. Many of those books talked about surviving
the process, which I could relate to because at
that time the essence, or context, of my grief was
definitely all about survival. However, ever since I
allowed myself to go into what seemed like a
huge abyss of grief associated with moving from
Seattle to Houston in 2003 and uprooting myself

from one community to another, and then with the death of my father in 2004, my experience of grief took on a completely different context. I shifted from relating to the grief process as something to survive, and instead began the journey of learning to relate to it as "sacred". By sacred, I mean giving reverence and respect to every precious moment and experience.

Until then, my opinion of grief was that it was inconvenient, overwhelming, and something to be managed or controlled. Grief certainly can be all of that and more. But in retrospect, what was missing for me was any regard or respect for the grief process and an unwillingness to consider that every moment during this extraordinary process, no matter how it occurred or felt, was sacred. Mostly how I related to what I was going through was as an adversary—like a child relates to naps. Grieving was a "have to," and by no means was it a choice or entered into willingly, recognizing it as a natural part of my life. My response was more like "I don't wanna!"

The truth of the matter is that for as long as I related to my grief in the not-so-friendly way I just described, I either suppressed or indulged it. I detached from it or was overwhelmed by it. Most of the time I was unwilling to just let it be and the emotional and physical impact over the course of 30 years was significant. Weight gain, weight loss, hair loss, insomnia, increased drinking, unresolved depression, physical exhaustion caused by a ferocious need to keep busy with anything that would distract me from dealing with whatever was happening, and relationships based primarily on my desire to escape the discomfort of pain, anxiety, and fear.

It would be naïve of me to think that I'm the only person on this planet to experience what I have just described. In fact, that's exactly why I'm writing this book. I am fairly confident that there are hundreds of thousands of people in the same boat, and it's sinking or anchored in a dark storm that doesn't seem to ever lift.

What qualifies me to write this book is not any special training or education in the arena of death, dying, or grief. I am by no means an educated expert on grief. However, what makes me the perfect person to explore *Sacred Grief* with you is that I am an ordinary person, perhaps just like you, who has experienced many losses and much grief. These losses varied in their circumstances, depth of pain, and duration. They encompassed early pregnancy, marriage, divorce, parenting, recovery from alcoholism, geographic moves, long periods of unemployment, deaths of friends, family members, and pets, and more recently the death of my father. So what I do know or, more accurately, what I have learned over time is that there are different ways that I can relate to grief, and ultimately I am the one who gets to choose and create that relationship.

Human beings experience all kinds of losses. The spectrum is vast: from losing a cherished possession or job, to the death of one's life-long partner, spouse, or beloved parent or child. The issue here is not that one is more intense or life-altering than another. The issue is that human beings tend to regard some losses as more sacred than others. This assessment or judgment is simply part of the human condition and an out-fall of having language. Unfortunately, as with most experiences, our preference for pleasure over pain has us subconsciously label and cate-gorize our losses, rather than consciously em-brace them all, treating each loss with the dignity and respect it deserves as part of the unique tap-estry of our lives.

It's so easy to try to strategize our way through grief. The desire to understand and con-trol life's endless ebb and flow is also part of the human condition. To a certain point, under-standing one's grief is valuable and makes a dif-ference. But somewhere we cross a line and on the other side of that line we have a lot of opin-ions about the process that are not particularly helpful in moving on with our lives. Instead, our judgments and strategies actually set the stage, or context, for our relationship to grief and the consequential self-induced suffering. I don't think this is an intentional thing. I just think it's human. But as human beings who have the capacity to observe and be aware of our inner dialogue, we have several choices when it comes to grief: resist it, indulge it, or choose the middle way—honor it, be awake to it, and allow it to unfold naturally with grace, beauty, and purpose.

Sacred Grief is about the middle way. The book explores consciously choosing the context for our grief and examines what's possible if we declare "sacred" as that context. If that were the case, then we wouldn't want to miss out on a single moment and we might experience our grief as more than just a process. Instead it would be an integral part of our life energy and existence. Now, that would be a profound context from which one could move through grief.

Sacred Grief is not a "how to" book. In fact, it probably won't take you long to realize that each chapter's discussion invariably leads you back to nothing. That's because it would be arrogant of me to even consider telling you how to create a relationship to your grief. Instead, *Sacred Grief* is a guide to exploring the possibility of your entire life as sacred, including the darkest, most difficult situations involving death and loss. And in that exploration, you take the opportunity to create an unimaginable relationship to grief as a friend who cares deeply for you, contributes to you, and supports you in living your life fully, and awake to every sacred moment.

A study guide of reflective questions for each chapter has been included in the Appendix to use in a group setting or while working with a therapist. My recommendation is that you read the entire book to gain the value of all the concepts presented before exploring and answering the questions. However, there is also value in turning to the study guide after you read each chapter and taking time to answer the questions before moving on to the next. Trust your instincts and follow your heart. Only you know what will serve you the most.

I don't know your grief or what has occurred in your life that had you pick up this book. You may have experienced far more losses than what I endured at a depth of pain that I cannot even begin to imagine. Or you may think that what you are going through pales in comparison to my story. It doesn't matter. Your grief, my grief, the world's grief—it's all sacred. For the mere fact that we exist and are going through whatever life has put in front of us, it's sacred. And it is no less sacred than the moments of delight and profound love and joy that life also throws our way.

We can relate to it all as sacred, or we can continue to pick and choose which losses we hold dearest. It's our choice and the choice we make, whether it's conscious or unconscious,

provides access to either peace or suffering. Today I invite you to choose the sacred path of
peace and honor it all.

Chapter 1
Sacred Surrender:
Leslee's Story

As I reflected on what to include in this book that would make a difference, it became clear to me that I needed to share my story. That's what this is all about—one person to another. Not an expert opinion, but an evolving human experience that spans trauma, denial, suppression, indulgence, awakening to, and at last the honoring of grief. As you read this story, I invite you to listen for the similarities. Many things will be different from your story, but I promise that if you listen for what's similar—as well as for what's possible—this story will make a difference for you.

My earliest recollection of a death was that of my grandfather when I was five years old. I was too young to really understand what was happening, and what I remember most is my parents and relatives being annoyed with me, my older sister, and cousins, and scolding our playful antics at the funeral home. I recall being intrigued with it all, but was mostly focused on laughing and whispering with the other children while sitting at the back of the room. I also have some recollection of things being moved from his home next door. However, the only sadness I remember came with the realization that my grandfather would no longer offer us gum or those delicious melt-in-your-mouth butter mints that we anticipated with much enthusiasm when we visited him.

Other early losses were goldfish that were either flushed down the toilet or wrapped in a tissue, placed in a small cardboard box, and with great dignity buried under a large violet bush in our backyard. A long legacy of parakeets also came and went, although I have little recollection of their actual deaths. The change in the color of feathers was the primary evidence that someone new occupied the cage. I can only assume that my mother or father lovingly handled all the details of their burial and a fresh specimen was quickly purchased to maintain harmony and minimize any upsets. It wasn't until my early adolescence that I experienced the first of a string of deaths and losses that would set the stage for what eventually became my primary relationship to grief.

My maternal grandmother, Rosalie, died when I was twelve years old. I had a very close and loving relationship with her. Although her Italian accent was heavy and I frequently had to guess at what she was saying, her love for our family and her affection and attention to my siblings and me was evident in the time she spent with us each summer. I remember being somewhat confused by the protocol that kept me from being near my mother at the funeral home the night before the service and burial. I could see that she was sad and felt compelled to be close and comfort her. She and her brothers and sisters sat in chairs up close to the casket and when I went to stand by her, someone gently moved me to where other relatives congregated.

The next day we were again at the funeral home before going to the church and cemetery. I was out in the hallway with my cousins and uncles when my grief hit. It came quickly, unexpectedly, and totally washed over me. I found myself weeping uncontrollably in the arms of an older cousin, embarrassed at the outbreak of tears and sobbing. The crying continued as we drove to the cemetery and during the graveside service. I don't remember when I finally stopped crying, but I did. I have no recollection of anyone telling me I shouldn't cry. In fact what I remember most is family who kept putting their arms around me, or holding my hand. However, since no one was talking to me about what was happening, I decided that I shouldn't talk about it either, so I pushed the emotions down and kept my thoughts to myself. From that point on I was fairly detached from my grief process.

Within the next eighteen months, I experienced three more significant losses—a childhood playmate, one of my girlfriends, and a young boy at school with whom I was just beginning to have a teen romance. Each died of different circumstances; one was in a car accident, one was violently murdered, and one drowned.

Although my reactions to the details of their deaths varied, I related to my grief with the same suppression and sense of detachment as I had with my grandmother's death. I wasn't aware of it, but my internal dialogue might have been something like, "Don't let anyone know how much you're hurting. Be strong." Or, "No one's asking you about it, so don't talk about it. They must not want to know." I suspect that these four deaths put firmly into place my relationship to grief—an emotion and force definitely to be suppressed and managed because if it weren't managed it would be overwhelming like it had been with my grandmother. The memory of the embarrassment and discomfort of that experience was still fresh and I definitely didn't want that to happen again.

I want to be clear that there is no blame to anyone about this, including myself. This is a human phenomenon that takes its course and that phenomenon is also part of the sacredness of one's life and grief. It went how it went, and the sacredness continues as my relationship to grief shifts and evolves. Those years and experiences are no less significant than my life is today.

Between the age of 18, when I moved 2,500 miles away from home to attend college, and my mid 30s, there would be many losses. Two babies lost in early pregnancy, three divorces, multiple job losses and extended periods of unemployment, the death of a beloved pet dog, and a daughter in recovery from drug addiction, followed by the confrontation of my codependency and addiction to alcohol. These experiences were interconnected and the catalyst for all the emotions identified in the grief process—sadness, anger, guilt, denial, and more. Remember, though, my relationship to grief was to manage it, so for years everything was suppressed and controlled.

Another loss during the same time period, although not associated with death, was the loss of my sense of safety and well-being after experiencing two rapes while in my mid-20s. These two incidents pushed me from being detached from my emotions to episodes of dissociation. The following years were lived in a "checked out" state of

being. In retrospect, it was like wandering in a
thick, heavy fog or being in a deep restless sleep.
The level of anger, shame, guilt, and self-disgust
that I felt was overwhelming. Any grief process
was completely out of my awareness and if it had
been something I could or chose to deal with, the
last word I would use to describe what I was going through would be sacred. In fact, if anyone
had even tried to approach me about relating to
my experience as sacred I would have lashed
back with anger and indignation.

With detachment and dissociation now as the
primary context to my life, I used a number of
behaviors to manage my grief—compulsive working, drinking, sex, smoking, eating, jogging, and
playing racquetball. I did everything in excess
with the primary intention to be anywhere except
where I was—in pain. I was always busy and on
the move, even during the periods of my life
when the compulsive behavior ceased or shifted
into a more normal state. I spent very little time
in quiet reflection, relaxing, or just "being" and
most of the time running from the experience of
whatever was going on in my life.

Given all of this and my response to a long
and difficult period of my life, my unwillingness
to show myself any kindness or compassion kept
me suffering and indulging in a non-stop internal
dialogue that had me desperately work to avoid
feeling my pain and anxiety. I pushed down

whatever I was feeling or checked out in any way that would give me some sense of order, rather than be with the ongoing sense of chaos, fear, and anxiety that was so prevalent for me.

In 1989, as I went through my third divorce, my world seemed to be falling apart and so was I. With some urgency for relief and help, I started attending a 12-Step program called Al-Anon, a support group for family members who are dealing with alcoholism and drug addiction. At the time, my teenage daughter was using drugs and alcohol to cope with her own emotions until we intervened and placed her in an adolescent treatment center. The stress of both situations spurred me to also seek out private therapy, a simple act that began the miraculous process of opening up to my life and the floodgates of my grief.

The urge here is to say that I started to honor the process. But truthfully, even with the depth of what was now consciously being given space to be, I still resisted relating to my grief as anything except inconvenient and unwanted. I wasn't willing to admit that, but it was definitely in the background of my grief. An older sister would later call that resistance "mischief" and that mischief unknowingly masked itself as victimhood, denial, self-indulgence, and self-pity.

These are harsh words and they describe someone fiercely caught up in an inner dialogue I wouldn't wish on my worst enemy. But it's the truth, and what I operated from for a very long time. My indulgence in the grief rather than just letting it be cost me countless moments of peace and resulted in a life void of any compassion for myself and an almost total lack of self-respect.

Somewhere around 1997, although more aware, yet still trying to control my emotions, I hit a wall. A sadness and depression settled over me that I couldn't seem to shake. I was still attending Al-Anon along with Alcoholics Anonymous to address my compulsive drinking and explore the source of my chaotic life and tightly-held resentments. I was hungry for peace and calm, and making headway towards living my life with less drama and instead more joy and harmony. Without realizing it, I had crossed a fine line between examining myself for the sake of curiosity and examining myself compulsively with an unconscious desire to once again be anywhere but where I was. In addition to hiding my pain, I desperately tried to manage the fear I was experiencing as a result of testing out new behavior, taking more risks in life, and dealing with life on life's terms. I was sober and completely conscious, with a commitment not to use any form of drugs, food, sex, or behavior to ease my emotional discomfort. It didn't matter whether I was feeling sadness and pain or excitement and fear.

None of it was considered sacred. It all just needed to be handled.

With the encouragement of one of my sisters, I went through a weekend-long personal growth program called the Landmark Forum. It's difficult to describe what occurred but there was actually a moment when I remember experiencing coming out of the thick fog I mentioned earlier and breaking free from my almost mechanical way of resisting any unpleasant and uncomfortable emotions. For the first time in my adult life I began to explore what was happening with curiosity instead of a desperate need to fix or change things. That year the door opened for me to start being with my life exactly as it was and to the grief that was patiently waiting to be acknowledged and moved through. I was now 45 years old.

My suffering diminished but I wasn't out of the woods yet. I still didn't realize that I could relate to everything I had experienced in my life as sacred. My opinions and judgments about my past were still running the show.

Five years later, in February 2003, life threw another curve ball. I had been in and out of work in Seattle for the previous two years and was offered a job in Houston. After much reflection and discussion with my family and friends, I decided to take the job and arrived in Houston three weeks later. Unfortunately, the job didn't work out and I resigned just five weeks after starting the job. Thrown by this unexpected turn of events within the brief span of eight weeks, I found myself in an exhilarating yet frightening freefall with several grief processes all mixed up. I was disappointed about how things had gone with the job, I now had no income, and I was grieving and adjusting to the move away from my family and friends in Seattle.

Fortunately for me, this time I was too physically and spiritually awake not to realize that whatever I was going though, even though it appeared "messy," was worthy of my attention. As much as I hated what I was going through—the pain, disappointment, fear, and self-doubt—I got it at a gut and heart level that this was my life and, not only was it precious, it was sacred.

With sacred as a new context for every moment and experience, I let my world fall apart and surrendered to having it all. I was nine years sober, so using alcohol or any other substance or behavior to "check out" wasn't an option. That left nothing to do but get in touch with the deep sadness, anger, and all the other emotions I was experiencing. I became interested in my grief and for the first time in my life I chose the middle way. I neither pushed anything away, nor indulged the process. I surrendered and stayed right where I was.

In the beginning there was so much emotional pain that my first reaction was to handle it and push my way through it as quickly as possible. Old habits die hard. But once again I couldn't ignore the strong urge to seek help and began working with a counselor in Houston. I kept waiting for the chance to rehash the past or analyze what was happening. I was pretty sure that would be the fastest way to eliminate the pain and anxiety and come out on the other side. Thankfully, my therapist had the professional training, common sense, and intuitive wisdom to make sure I did not go down that path. She told me that her job was to check in with me about what I was doing to take of myself and to help me let my world fall apart. Being strong was not going to carry the day.

At first I came to our sessions annoyed and angry, and then I surrendered again—to her wisdom and support. Each week I would tell her what I had done to take care of myself. She would mostly ask questions. Was I reaching out to others? Was I sleeping? What was I eating? Was I exercising? We did this until we were both sure that I had stabilized in the midst of my freefall. Then I was on my own again, awake and watching wide-eyed with curiosity and peace (at last!) the unfolding and rearrangement of my life as I once knew it. That was when things really got interesting because for the first time, I began to have a friendly relationship not just to my life, but to my grief.

Over the course of the next two years I would say that I began to relate to my grief in the same way that I had begun to relate to people. I became willing to let trust grow. I also became willing to let it teach and soften me, rather than to focus on what I could prove about myself and how strong I was. It was unimaginable for me to consider that my grief and I could be friends. But that is exactly what happened.

Just because you become friends with your life or grief, doesn't mean you stop experiencing difficulties and challenges. I remained unemployed for the next year and finances continued to be shaky. Temporary job assignments, although not offering the benefits of a fulltime position, allowed me to physically, emotionally, and spiritually heal. I became curious about Houston and ventured out to explore my new surroundings. There were moments of anxiety and confusion, as I learned the ins and outs of the two loops (freeway systems) that surround this gigantic city. I slept a lot and walked almost daily around a local park. I volunteered at church to get more connected to my new spiritual home. I read and re-read some of my favorite novels. And I cried.

When I wasn't working, I took time to move through the grief. I paid as much attention to when I felt anger and guilt, as I did to when I felt sad and lonely. I also paid attention to the moments when I sat outside by the pool reading and felt completely at peace. I got to have it all by giving up my right to discern which emotion I was friendly with and which I was not. It was the perfect training ground to prepare me for having my world rocked when my father died less than two years later.

I was just catching my breath from the challenges of the two previous years. I was working fulltime and my finances were finally stabilizing. I was feeling settled, had made some new friends, and felt at ease and completely at home in Houston. One Friday night, my brother called while I was working my way through traffic and trying, without much success, to drive to San Antonio for the funeral of a friend's brother the next day. It was one of those calls you dread getting. My dad had a close call. They thought he'd had a heart attack. The doctors were talking about putting in some stents, and my brother would know more later. We discussed whether or not I should come home. In retrospect, I think we both didn't want to deal with how serious the situation might be. His first response was that I should wait.

We spoke again shortly after that and decided that I should come home. While I was talking to him, I couldn't help but notice that the tangled traffic was not letting me get out of town. So I turned my car around and headed home to call the airlines and get on a plane to Wisconsin as soon as possible. The next morning I was on the first flight out and spent the next few days helping care for my dad while he was in the hospital. My memories of that time are vivid. Not so much because of his death, but because I kept choosing to stay present and honor each moment as sacred. Never before have I consciously experienced so much intimacy and fear at the same time.

The stents were put in and my father was sent home two days later with the prospect of feeling stronger. At home he continued to be short of breath and we were all concerned when that didn't seem to improve. The doctor assured us it was part of what we were dealing with because of the heart disease. The last day I was there, and the last time I saw my dad, I sensed his fear at not being able to catch his breath. I helped him get out of bed that morning and get dressed. I made both him and my mom breakfast and then gave them a little pep talk before heading off to the airport. I held on a little tighter and longer when hugging him.

I don't think I really thought it would be the last time I would hug or see him, but I had gotten scared that weekend and was a bit more present to his mortality. Even in the hospital, while moistening his lips, helping him eat, or helping untangle all the tubes and contraptions that were connected to him, I paid close attention to everything possible—his hands, the feel of his skin, his eyes, his hair—to commit it to memory. I wanted every precious moment those few days to be sacred and honor him for the great man and father he was in my life. I returned to Houston at peace that I had been the kind of daughter I had always wanted to be, and perhaps the kind of person he was proud to call his daughter.

A week later he was back in the hospital. His breath was still short and he was weak. The idea was to have him regain his strength, as well as give my mother some support in caring for him. She was 80 and having a hard time doing all that needed to be done at home for him. Another week passed and it was Thanksgiving. I was spending the holiday with a friend's family in San Antonio—a true blessing given my concern about being away from my dad and family when things were so uncertain about his health. I called him on Thanksgiving and we spoke briefly. He was tired and wanted to rest. Our conversation lasted less than five minutes. It would be our last.

By the end of the weekend he grew weak. Each time I called he was either having some kind of test done, sleeping, or resting and unable to talk. I became frustrated and concerned. There were signs that he was becoming weaker rather than stronger and everyone was concerned. Our entire family was there with him through the weekend except a younger brother and me. I started to consider flying home and let my boss know I might have to take off for home on short notice.

By Monday night my father's kidneys began to fail. A late afternoon conversation with an older sister had me wondering if this was it. By ten o'clock that evening she called, crying. "You should come," she said. Things were happening quickly and she wasn't sure if he would last another day.

I fought the urge to panic and called a friend. She offered to make calls to rearrange my schedule while I called the airlines. I had a hard time focusing on what the reservation person was saying but somehow managed to make flight arrangements and write down all the information. The last flight to Milwaukee that evening was about to leave and although I desperately wanted to be on it, I couldn't get to the airport before it took off. Instead I surrendered and began to make arrangements to get to the airport early the following day. I thought morning would never come and breathed a deep sigh of relief when I finally boarded the plane the next morning.

The flying time from Houston to Milwaukee, with a connection, is almost four hours. That's a lot of time in which to reflect, worry, pray, and stay present. I was grateful for a single aisle seat towards the front with seats occupied only behind me. Not having passengers on either side made it a little easier to let myself cry when the tears welled up. As we approached our first and only stop in Chicago, the plane shuddered. I couldn't help but wonder if something had just happened to my dad.

We landed and I walked off the plane. I couldn't bring myself to call my sister just yet so I stopped at Starbucks, got some coffee and called a good friend who knew the pain of losing a parent. I wasn't ready to face the possibility that he had died. We talked a bit and then I walked down to the gate to make my next connection. Still not ready to face what might be news of his death, I stopped to get a sandwich and soft drink. I made my way to the gate, sat down, began to eat, pulled out my cell phone and dialed my sister's number. I had taken a few bites of the sandwich and was chewing slowly. It wasn't going down easily, my throat felt so tight. I was afraid. My sister answered right away and without pausing, very lovingly told me that my father had died about 30 minutes before I landed. That's when the fog set in.

The rest of our conversation seemed like a slow motion dream from which I couldn't wake up. I asked some questions, and kept chewing my food. Tears started to roll down my cheeks

and I became aware of someone watching me. I
think that person knew I was getting bad news,
as he had a look of compassion and concern on
his face. He wasn't intruding. He was just being
with me. I finished the call with my sister and
made plans for my brother to pick me up in Milwaukee when I landed. Then I hung up and was
left with just me.

I don't think I will ever forget that moment.
Here I was, in this huge airport, not knowing a
single person, and feeling completely vulnerable
and intimate with everyone and everything. I sat
for a moment, swallowed hard to get down the
last of my sandwich, and then walked over to a
bank of pay phones and called my friend again. I
didn't want to be with only strangers when I felt
the pain I no longer could avoid—didn't want to
avoid. She answered, I told her my dad had died,
that I hadn't made it there to be with him, and
then I laid my head against the cold metal of the
phone and sobbed. There was nothing else to do.

I don't remember anything about the last
connection to Milwaukee. I don't even remember
walking off the plane and going to baggage claim.
There isn't anything in my memory until I walked
outside to wait for my brother. I remember the
air was quite cold—much colder than Houston is
in November. It was November 30th and my father had died. My brother arrived moments later
and we began the 40-minute drive from the air-

port to my parents' home. I am blessed with brothers who aren't afraid to cry. This brother, Jim, and I cried together as we drove, made our customary stop for coffee, and then climbed back in the car for the remainder of the drive. It seemed to take longer than usual, and the anxiety and sadness increased as we got close to city limits and my parents' home. I didn't know what it was going to be like when I walked in the door and my father wasn't there to greet me or to give me a hug. When we pulled up in the driveway, for a moment I didn't want to go in. I didn't have to remember the thought "Sacred. It's all sacred". It was just there. There would be no escape, because I said so.

Even though that next entire week felt like I was caught in the midst of a heavy fog, I remember it all. I remember poignant moments of tenderness with my mother as she described her last moments with her husband. I remember the anxiety as we headed to the funeral home to arrange the service and select his casket—a handsome oak work of art that would be a tribute to his life as a skilled and talented carpenter. I remember the stomachaches I felt while selecting flowers with my mother and sister for the funeral home and again later as we sifted through photos and created collages depicting his life, family, and friends. There were moments when my sister went to make some soup, my mother and other siblings were off doing other things, and I was left to clip and paste photos with only my sadness.

Along with deep sadness was disbelief and exhaustion. After returning from the viewing at the funeral home and several hours of greeting good friends and close family members, I couldn't wait to go to bed. I didn't sleep well, but there was this point of exhaustion from being with it all. My daughter, who had arrived from Seattle, and I slept in the bed my father had slept in. No one else seemed to want to use that room and, as far as I was concerned, it was the perfect place in which to be with my father's memory: his clothes, talcum powder, coins, cuff links, and little stacks of "stuff" that were evidence that he had once been there.

I am frequently amazed at the peacefulness that surrounded our family during this time. There were no arguments. We naturally deferred to our mother when it came to final decisions about funeral arrangements and details. It was almost as if how we were all being was as peaceful as I've been told my father was at the end of his life. He had surrendered and let go. He wasn't afraid. He was done living and ready to move on with the next adventure and mystery. The rest of us would have the same task as we moved into our individual experiences of life without him. His act of dying was an inspiration and an exam-

ple of a powerful way from which to live. In the
end he was friendly with his death. Rather than
resist it, he moved toward the mystery and unknown of the next sacred moment.

Chapter 2
Just the Facts Ma'am:
Separating Fact from Fiction

If we are interested in having an uncondi-
tional relationship with our grief, surrendering to
sacredness over and over again, we need to start
from nothing. To get to nothing, we need to separate reality from illusion. However, most of us
wouldn't consciously give grief this kind of consideration. We hardly take the time to separate
reality from illusion with our friends and loved
ones. Why on earth would we want to take the
time to sort all that out as it relates to our grief?

Well, for starters, just as with others, a relationship to grief based on illusions or myths can
lead to disappointment, upsets, and frustration
and frequently promotes more suffering than
peace. When I say myths I'm not referring to the
work that has been done to define the tasks and
stages of grief. Those aren't myths. They are ob-

servations from countless hours of professional counseling and research. The myths I'm talking about come mostly from us. They are the stories we tell ourselves along the way to avoid or ease the pain, like:

- I should be over this by now.
- It shouldn't hurt this much.
- If I give in to my pain it will never end.
- If I cry, that will mean I'm weak.
- I have to be strong so that I don't upset others.
- Men don't cry.
- I should know how to handle all these feelings.

The harsh fact about these myths is that, rather than ease our pain, they actually add to it. Furthermore, as long as we believe that they are true, we will create a barrage of self-induced suffering that grossly exceeds what the natural process indiscriminately gives us. The suffering arises when we assess where we are in the process, how we are handling it, and who is or isn't comforting us, blah, blah, blah. Here's how it goes

We start to feel some emotion and automatically decide whether it's good or bad. If it's what we label bad, we push the sensation down to protect ourselves rather than allow it to come and go. Then we create a thought, or myth, to explain to ourselves why we shouldn't feel what we're feeling. Our need to understand then becomes more important than experiencing what's happening because we're convinced understanding is the means to avoid the pain. But the pain hasn't passed and sooner or later the sensation returns and the whole cycle of judging, suppressing, and trying to understand what's happening starts all over again. Now, piled on top of the pain, is the deep, constricting ache of suffering rather than the peace of allowing the pain to just "be."

Given what I've just described, the whole idea of fabricating or buying into myths is insane. But we can't stop the insanity or suffering until we take responsibility for creating it. Only then are we left with "just the facts, ma'am" about the natural unfolding of our grief and here are some of those facts.

1. Grief presents us with a vast array of emotions human beings typically label negative. These emotions include pain, sadness, depression, confusion, frustration, guilt, blame, and anger.

2. Grief also presents us with an array of emotions human beings typically label positive. These emotions include relief, love, forgiveness, and peace.

3. The grief process is not linear. It ebbs and flows and is as flexible as life itself and as

you and I. It is neither stagnant nor con-
strained to being any particular way.

4. Grief has no sense of time or space. It has
   no concern with a schedule or way of being
   expressed.

5. Grief is as much a part of our natural lives
   as the bliss of falling in love, the profound
   moment of childbirth, the sensual experience of lovemaking, or the satisfaction and
   delight of having a dream manifest itself in
   reality.

6. Grief is not selective about who gets to experience it. No one is exempt.

7. Grief holds no human being more or less
   capable of moving through its process than
   another.

If any of these facts sound familiar it's because they are as relevant to life as they are to
grief. Everything comes and goes. Just as pain
comes and goes, so does joy and every emotion
in-between. In each waking moment, human beings shift and change. Rarely are we in the same
mood or state of being at the end of the day that
we start with in the morning. If we relate to grief
the same way we relate to the people in our lives,
with expectations based on our illusions or
myths rather than how they are in any given

moment, we are left with an experience of suffering created by no one but ourselves.

So, what is it that would allow us to create a relationship to grief that is not based on myth? Well, first of all, as I mentioned earlier in this chapter, we need to take responsibility for the assessments that constantly cross our minds. Then we give up our attachment to the decisions and past experiences that led to those assessments and rest comfortably in "don't know." Buddhists call this empty mind, or beginner's mind. It is the space of creation where anything is possible and the perfect breeding ground from which to create a completely new relationship to grief. One that is not based on myths, but one that shifts and flows with the natural, universal wisdom and knowledge inherent in the grief process.

Now let's explore this deeper. If we are creating this relationship from nothing and we have language, we can use that language to create a thought or idea that enhances our lives rather than adds to our suffering. That thought or idea then becomes the "context" to our experience. I address context at length in the next chapter but touched briefly on it in my story when I described driving up to my parents' home after arriving for the funeral. I was afraid to go inside and the thought that came to mind was "Sacred. It's all sacred." I can't really explain why that particular thought was there, but it doesn't matter. What matters is that I now had an idea—a context—that could surround all the ensuing events. I didn't want to miss out on a single moment because I wanted to honor and respect my father and this celebration of his life and death.

Another thought or idea that makes a difference when it comes to relationships is "conscious commitment." Relationships flourish and expand when there is a commitment that has us stay with someone or something for its natural duration. We have many relationships we maintain at different levels of commitment: co-workers, neighbors, friends, parents, children, siblings, and so on. Many of our daily interactions have an automatic quality to them. We don't think about how we are going to interact with the postman, grocery store clerk, or beautician. When we see them we say, "Hello." "How are you?" "Have a nice day." "Take care," and then go on our way.

Then there are other relationships in our lives where, to some degree or another, we are aware of our commitment. These relationships include spouses, partners, children, and close friends. They don't just come and go and we are completely clear that we are "in" these relationships. We invest time and energy with the intention to deepen and sustain them and they are the relationships that we may already relate to as "sacred." They contribute to us, we contribute to them, and it is because of this that we actually remain in these relationships.

Consider what life would be like if we were consciously committed to all our relationships. They would take on many different forms but we would be genuinely interested in and respect the other person exactly as they are in every moment. This conscious commitment would bring a curious quality to every interaction with whoever happened to be there in that moment—the kind of curiosity experienced when one holds a sleeping baby and notices with awe its tiny features and peaceful presence.

If we can believe that it's possible to commit this way to every relationship in our lives, it follows that we could choose to consciously commit to anything in our lives, including to our grief. It would also follow that if we are completely committed then we could also learn to trust, respect, and accept our grief. Like our other relationships, it would have a beginning and an end, ups and downs, moments of sheer confusion and frustration, and moments of pure ecstasy and joy. If all of that is possible out of just declaring a conscious commitment to our grief, what would have us so adamantly resist that which has the capacity to bring healing and peace to our lives?

Remember my story and the early decision I made to suppress my grief when my grandmother died? In retrospect, I can see that I also operated from that same experience and decision in my personal relationships. I began to suppress my feelings and not share about them with the people in my life. Rather than act from a conscious commitment to those relationships, I was still compensating for an extremely uncomfortable experience in the past. Granted, I was a child and my choice back then, although unconscious, was logical. But today I'm not a child dealing with my grandmother's death. I'm an adult who is capable of making conscious choices about who and what I am committed to now.

And so it is with all of us. We are all completely capable of giving up our attachment to the young decisions we made that created reference points that no longer serve us. We then come face-to-face with the dilemma all human beings face. Given the fact that there are endless beginnings and endings throughout our lives, we have to grapple with the reality that grief demands a considerable portion of our time and energy. It happens frequently and takes on many forms: divorce, lost jobs, broken relationships, death, retirement, watching your 5-year-old get on the bus for their first day of school, watching your 18-year-old go off to college or your children get married, or perhaps having a loved one go off to war and never return alive.

All of these events present us with the opportunity to recognize our grief and move through it, sometimes quickly and sometimes slowly. It is frequently there and right alongside the grief is the opportunity to choose how we are going to relate to the spectrum of emotions that begin to ebb and flow. We can also declare our commitment to the grief process. Am I in or am I out? Will I push and strategize my way through this as quickly as possible or will I latch onto my grief with the grip of death and indulge it for all it's worth? Am I open to taking the middle way, not grasping nor indulging, and let the sensations come and go? Am I willing to honor it for as long as we both shall live?

This moment will present itself many times over and each time we can choose to step into the unknown and vast space of nothing. When we work with the facts, our reference point for what is occurring is nothing and we can create anything. When we work with what is happening based on our past decisions and self-created myths, the reference point is our opinions, assessments, and predictions. One path breeds peace, the other breeds suffering. Which path will you choose the next time grief enters your life?

Chapter 3
The Power of Language: Declaring "Sacred" as a Context

There is no difference in the sacredness of our losses unless we say so. That's a bold statement given that the depth of pain and impact of losing a child cannot and does not begin to compare with losing a job. That's not what I'm saying. I want to be very clear here, so let me say it again. There is no difference in the sacredness of our losses. Since this book is called *Sacred Grief*, let's explore declaring "sacred" as a context.

Webster's Dictionary defines sacred as "made or declared holy" and holy is defined as "deserving or regarded with special reverence or respect." Given those definitions, declaring "sacred" as the context for our grief would have every single moment of the process, no matter how painful or peaceful, receive the same level of reverence and attention. There would also be no need to assess where we are in the process as we move through its natural life. There would, instead, be a friendly and compassionate quality to our observations about each day's events and how we are responding. We would be as curious about our grief as we are when we watch small infants learn to walk, talk, and express themselves. The process would not be without pain, nor would it be without joy. Rather than prefer one emotion over another, we would respect and welcome it all.

Unfortunately, human beings don't normally operate from these ideas. In fact, in the Western world the words "grief" and "sacred" rarely come together in the same sentence. A more typical description of the process might be inconvenient, unpredictable, overwhelming, and annoying. God forbid we should set aside our normal happy lives to deal with grief.

The trouble with the perception of a "normal happy life" is that if we are honest with ourselves, rarely are we consistently happy. Being happy is a state of mind that comes and goes and so is being disappointed, delighted, irritated, and depressed. Along with these everyday emotions are the experiences of being sad, angry, anxious, and the entire spectrum of emotions associated with grief. We can do all kinds of things to avoid certain emotions or sensations that we find uncomfortable, but it doesn't really matter.

Everything comes and goes, including pain and pleasure. However, if we are willing to respect every moment of our lives as sacred, then every sensation or experience would be given space to just "be".

In the case of grief, our initial reaction to finding ourselves in this process might be fear, anger, or dread. It's as if we brace ourselves for something that hasn't happened yet, but we are absolutely certain that it's going to be horrible. Then, as we begin to experience our grief, we complain to ourselves and our friends that it's taking too long, it shouldn't be this hard, we should be over it by now, or we shouldn't be so emotional—all those myths we discussed earlier. Rarely are we willing to entertain the idea that this whatever-we've-labeled-it process just might contribute to us, heal us, and soften us into more compassionate human beings.

Why do you suppose that is?

Well, to get to the heart of this issue, we have to be open to the idea that we already have a relationship with our grief. Since that relationship is mostly based on our myths and critical assessments, you could say that our relationship to grief is somewhat aggressive and unfriendly. That would make complete sense because grief is probably the last thing we would welcome and choose to go through if we actually got to pick and choose what life throws our way. But there

are many situations that we don't get to choose
and instead they are a natural outfall of life. Stuff
happens—natural disasters, traumatic events,
incomprehensible criminal acts. So, the choice
then becomes not so much about what life
throws our way, but rather how we work with or
relate to it.

In the previous chapter, I introduced the idea
of creating a context—an idea surrounding our
words and conversations that impacts our experience of people, places, and things. If there
were no context to our relationships we would be
detached and mechanical in our communications
and interactions. Like animals, we would just
"be." There would actually be some benefit to
that, and the "being" part is the primary focus of
what I'm getting at here. But remember, unlike
animals, human beings have language which
leads to forming an opinion or decision about
what's happening. In doing so, it could be said
that the decision or opinion itself becomes the
context of our relationship to whatever's happening.

Now let's take it a step further and explore the
impact such a context would have on a relationship. Suppose the context for your relationship to
your best friend was based on your ongoing assessments of what that person said or did. Every
time the two of you spoke or interacted, what
would be hanging out in the background (your

inner dialogue) is some form of "She's crazy." "He doesn't know what he's talking about." "I don't like what she just said (or did) so I shouldn't be friends with her," or "I agree with what she just said, so it's okay. We can still be friends."

As silly as that all sounds, it's not too far off from what goes on in our heads. We all do this and left unchecked the non-stop chatter can leave us feeling exhausted, lead to frequent disagreements and to a back-and-forth, on-the-fence quality to our relationships. "Am I in or am I out? Are they in or are they out? Will he leave me? I'd better not talk about what I'm really feeling because I might upset him and then he might go away."

There is no give and take, there is no contribution, and there is no freedom for either person to be just the way they are in that moment. The result of a context based on judging and assessing is a lot of noise and self-induced suffering. You know exactly what I'm talking about when I say self-induced suffering. It's that endless inner pain and turmoil that colors our thoughts, words, and actions. It takes a lot of energy to work with this kind of relationship. It's not good or bad, it's just exhausting.

Now let's look at it from a different angle. In this scenario, your relationship with your best friend is based on mutual love and respect. You might even go so far as to say that the context of the relationship is sacred. That would mean that every time the two of you spoke or interacted, you would hold your friend in high regard. No moment or experience would be exempt from being considered within this context.

Can you imagine what that would be like? If you can't imagine what it would be like, just notice that the idea of it is so profound that it's almost unimaginable. So, let's play with this idea. I'm going to assert that relating to your friendship as sacred would leave very little room for strategizing, manipulating, controlling, or dominating. The relationship would be based on mutual respect and the freedom to be fully self-expressed. No one would interfere with or question the other's desire to be a particular way in any given moment. The relationship would be perfect. There would still be things to deal with and work out, but the perfection would be in the workability of the relationship just the way it is.

So how do you apply these same concepts to your relationship to grief? First of all, let's suppose you were to set aside all judgment about whatever the loss was, and if you noticed yourself judging it, you would stop that. The habit of judging would be intentionally replaced by a practice of acknowledging all losses as sacred. Then let's suppose you were willing to start working with the grief in its natural state, just the way it is. The grief comes when it comes, hurts when it hurts, and enlightens when it enlightens. It also brings you to your knees when it brings you to your knees, and shifts and moves when it shifts and moves. You don't get in the way of grief's self-expression. You let it be and you welcome and respect it like a cherished friend. Now that would be a profound and unimaginable relationship with grief. Possible? Absolutely. However, going from the unimaginable to the possible happens only after one is willing to release the old context and surrender to something new and unfamiliar.

Although it's only a word, context, in and of itself, is a powerful distinction and worthy of further discussion. If you work in any arena that deals with the impact of the spoken or written word, you can appreciate the value and power of context when composing such things as advertising campaigns, speeches, articles, and theatrical plays. In fact stage performances are an excellent example of this concept. They involve the critical setting of a scene; defining everything around the actors and in the background that deliberately pulls the audience into the story or plot. You might even say that by setting the stage—or context—the playwright defines the relationship between the audience and what's happening. How well that relationship is defined and communicated can make or break a play's success. This is evidenced by the theatrical overnight flops and successes we hear about every day.

The same is true in our lives. Life provides the players, and all the details—who, what, when, and where—of our experiences. Life happens on its own terms and we're thrown into the mix of players. Now, since life itself doesn't have language, life can't set the context for the relationship between ourselves and what's happening. But we can. In fact, whether we realize it or not, that's exactly what we do. The value in exploring this concept is getting clear that because we have language there is always a context to our relationship to the events in our lives. It doesn't matter whether that context is created consciously or unconsciously. However, the minute we become conscious of our ability to "set the stage" for our lives—and for our grief—it becomes crystal clear that the context we operate from is determined by none other than *moi*, me, you, ourselves. Consequently, if there is going to be a context to our lives and, in this case, to our grief, it just might behoove us to create one that fosters a friendly relationship to this important process.

I can tell you with confidence that the primary benefit of consciously choosing to have a sacred and friendly relationship to grief is the reduction, if not almost complete elimination, of unnecessary self-induced suffering. If we relate to what we are going through with respect and trust, there is only the doubting and questioning that arise naturally rather than the non-stop internal dialogue in which we tend to indulge. I can also assure you that declaring a sacred context to one's grief is not about fixing, understanding, or taking away the uncomfortable sensations that naturally arise. However, with "sacred" as the context, there lives the possibility of peacefully moving through our pain and discomfort without causing additional pain to ourselves or others.

There are many aspects of grief's journey that we dislike. I personally don't like how my eyes get all red and puffy when I cry. Shortly after my father died, I would put on makeup in the morning and on my way to work I'd drive along the same road I was traveling when my brother first called. I'd remember all that occurred back then and begin to cry. By the time I got to the office building my makeup was gone—washed away—and I would wear my sunglasses so that no one would notice how I looked as I rode the elevator up 73 stories. When I finally got to my desk, I would reapply my makeup and get on with the day.

Even now, three years later, I am still annoyed with the inconvenience of this scenario but I stay with the pain and sadness. I let the sensations come and go because they are sacred and arise out of a deep love for my father. Why would I want to be anywhere other than where I am in that moment?

Well, one reason we want to be somewhere else other than with our pain is because feeling grief's deep pain can be physically uncomfortable as well as frightening. Sometimes what we experience seems to squeeze and contract the heart so hard that breathing is difficult. The throat and chest tighten as the pain wells up and starts to work itself through the body. The tendency for human beings, particularly in the Western world, is to resist this pain or sensation. There is an almost automatic pulling back, especially when the pain is intense.

For me, rather than pull back, I do what I did when my father first died. I think, "Sacred. It's all sacred.' and then breathe and allow the pain to pass. Sometimes I have the sensation of being completely washed over or having the wind knocked out of me. When that happens the pain can literally bring me to my knees. I have two adorable brown tabby cats that get quite curious when this happens and then come close to comfort me. It amazes me how perceptive and loving they are without using language to express themselves. They just "be" with me, and the whole experience becomes humorous as well as beautiful.

Relating to grief as sacred is like watching a fabulous epic drama of my life unfold and I'm the star! I become curious and interested in each scene, and want to stay with it to the very end.

Then things lighten up and I find myself enter-
tained, energized, and surprisingly content.

Chapter 4
The Pitfalls of Preferences

The primary obstacle to human beings being content with the moment is language. Without language, everything would just be. We would be back to being like babies before they learn to talk, noticing everything with curiosity. Babies just take it all in and "go with the flow." When they're hungry they cry and then eat, when they are tired they sleep, and when they wake up they are ready to take in some more.

But we're adults who have learned to prefer pleasure over pain so it's not that simple anymore. Whether we like it or not, we cannot escape the fact that life has its own ebb and flow, and it shifts and turns with unpredictable speed. It's been wisely said that the only thing constant in life is change—a fact that most human beings tend to resist. Instead, we think that we have some better idea of how our lives are supposed to go. We think this a lot, if not all the time, and therein lies the first pitfall: habitual judging and assessing.

We've already discussed our compulsive tendency to judge and assess our experiences and the sensations we feel. Now let's take a look at the habitual aspect of this behavior. Webster's Dictionary defines habit as "an often involuntary pattern of behavior acquired by frequent repetition." There are many things we do in our daily lives that have an involuntary or automatic quality to them: driving the same route to work every day, making coffee, taking a shower, getting ready for work, or walking the dog. These are the routine tasks we execute to take care of ourselves and to function in the communities where we live, work, and play.

Over time, we start to do one thing while doing another and frequently don't even notice what we're doing. Instead, we might think about the fight we had with our boss while walking the dog or discuss dating with our teenager while getting dressed for work. What begins as a deliberate action or practice eventually becomes a habit. In the beginning we gave thought and intention to what we were saying or doing, and then we stopped paying attention. Our life is full of these habits, each contributing some type of quality to our lives, depending on the nature of the activity.

It's like that with habitual judging and assessing. What starts out as a childlike practice of being curious about and exploring life, over time turns into an automatic habit of categorizing and labeling. The shift happens with the introduction of language and labeling: good, bad; right, wrong; pleasure, pain. Once the labeling becomes a habit, it becomes a pitfall because the space for curiosity gets smaller and smaller until there is only our imagined "truth." Also, if we are constantly evaluating our lives based on how we think they should or shouldn't be, there is no being here now, in the present moment. We are either judging what's happening based on the past or imagining a future that's pleasurable because it's better to be happy than sad. Can you start to see the pitfall?

Then, all of a sudden, life takes one of its unexpected turns. Someone you deeply love dies, a marriage ends, or a child disappears. The unthinkable happens and without realizing it we fall back to our habit of judging and assessing. It gets even more poignant when the word grief is spoken—especially in the Western world. Unlike other parts of the world that instinctively honor every moment and emotion that comes with grief, the Western world operates differently. I'm not saying that it should be any different than this. In fact, the world is going to go the way it's going to go, and we are going to die when we are going to die. However, my instincts and experience tell me that something else is possible other than relating to grief based on one's incessant assessment of the process.

If we declare that we are not going to miss out on a single moment of our lives, it would behoove us to use language to create a relationship to grief that has us be here now. If we can create judgments and assessments, we can create sacredness. The choice is up to us. In fact, it's more than up to us. There isn't anyone else. It's up to you. You get to say, and you are the only one who can say how your grief is going to be for you. That's a fact, and if you can accept that fact, then you are on your way out of the storm of unnecessary, self-induced suffering and into a peace that transcends all understanding.

Another pitfall that prevents us from being content with the moment is our desire for pain to be short-lived. We have this illusion that we can control the duration of our pain and prefer it to go away as quickly as possible. When the pain sensation comes up, we resist its presence and invariably delay its natural movement and progress. Depending on the depth of our loss, our resistance can go on for years and the delayed grief actually increases rather than reduces our suffering. Delayed or unresolved grief ends up being more intense than the original pain, and what might naturally take a year to process, may take much longer.

When I first experienced the grief from my three divorces, I truly thought that it would never end. I gave a fair amount of time and energy to that thought (or myth) and ended up adding to what was already a difficult situation. I was always questioning when the pain and sadness would stop and then, rather than just experience it, I got resigned to it. Once I became resigned to it, I began to indulge it. The pain and suffering unconsciously became a context to my life rather than a normal part of the process. Thus began a long period of self-induced suffering that I wasn't willing to be responsible for until many years later.

In retrospect, I'm certain that how I responded back then was logical, given my frame of mind and how I was consumed by my circumstances rather than observing them. Today I don't have any regrets or judgment about that time of my life. Accepting and making peace with how things went has been part of my journey and process. But I also know that today, given a different frame of mind and the willingness to be curious about my life, I could have responded differently and instead allowed the process to unfold naturally.

I've noticed that since I declared "sacred" as the context for my grief, most of the time my emotions move through me with surprising speed and ease. They might come up at times I consider inconvenient (at work, at the gym while working out, while I'm standing in line at the bank), but if I keep my mind quiet, my heart open, and breathe, the emotion or sensation passes. When I reflect on my grief process since November 2004 when my father died, there have probably been as many moments of pain, anger and sadness as there have been moments when I've felt happy, bored, calm, and relaxed. I can honestly say that I have experienced and honored it all, and reaped the rewards of choosing to relate to it all as sacred.

What's even more interesting is that the attention I've paid to relating to my grief as sacred has strengthened that muscle, so to speak, in all areas of my life. When situations occur that might have me doubt, judge, or resist what's happening, I stay open and curious. There might be some uncomfortable emotion—whatever the situation has pushed up—but instead of creating additional suffering, I let the sensation be and then move on to the next moment. Unlike the past, I don't find myself wanting to be happy all the time. Rather I'm satisfied and content with whatever sensation I'm experiencing. Sometimes happiness is the sensation of the moment, hour or day, and sometimes it's not. There is a new faith in life and a strengthening of my trust in its natural unfolding. Just as in our relationships with human beings, establishing and building trust takes first a willingness to have trust grow, and then patience to allow it to grow. My experience is that the willingness and patience is a natural outfall of staying in and being content with the moment, just the way it is.

There are moments when I wonder if it should really be this easy. Sometimes I even think I'm weird for the lack of drama and additional suffering that was once so prevalent in my life. I'm willing to be curious about that, too, rather than suffer about it. Those moments are sacred; they pass and a new moment arises.

The last pitfall I want to discuss is such a pervasive part of our everyday language that I think it deserves some attention. It's the opinion or myth we might have that because women are more in touch with their emotions, they are better at grieving than men.

Historically, research tells us that men and women's brains are wired differently and that one sex has greater access to emotions than the other. The Western world has responded to that research with many books that explore and explain these differences. I agree with the notion that women are wired differently, but that doesn't mean they have more access to their emotions than men. Some women might be more open to what they're feeling, but both genders have the capacity to access their emotions. I have known men that can identify their feelings and are willing to be authentic and express those feelings without any prying or cajoling. I have also known women who are immensely comfortable primarily with happiness and anger. Lastly, I have known women who are exceptionally grounded in their femininity and yet stopped by the fear of consciously moving forward in the grief process after a difficult loss. They will be the first to tell you that they are not going there.

I am moved by what I just described because, in each case, these people have transcended the research regarding gender. What they are or are not willing to express and share becomes a human issue rather than a gender issue. Instead they are being authentic and, from my perspective, being authentic not only lives but flourishes in the world of "sacred."

Chapter 5
Mischief:
Grief's Masquerade

In life, frequently what we think we're feeling isn't what we're really feeling. Emotional sensations have a tendency to occur as something other than what they really are. For some of us that might equate to being nice when we are angry, crying when we actually want to lash out in anger, or smiling or laughing when we are sad. Sometimes we are aware this is happening, and sometimes we're not. We might also equate this phenomena with the challenge to identify a sensation or feeling. We get so comfortable with being nice or angry, or feeling guilty or worthless, that eventually every sensation is colored by those feelings. To express some other emotion is so foreign that we just can't go there—consciously or unconsciously.

It can be like that with grief. I don't really know what the psychological mechanism is that is behind one feeling masquerading as another, so for the sake of this discussion let's call this phenomena mischief.

My personal experience of mischief at play has sometimes lasted for years within a period of grief. When I uncovered the true emotion, I was astounded at the depth of self-induced suffering that went completely unnoticed, keeping at bay the natural unfolding of my grief and healing. As such it deserves discussion and attention, so let's play with an analogy to get clear about what I mean by mischief.

Suppose you live in Chicago and you decide you want to drive to New York. You've never been there before, so you look at a map and see that you have to take a particular route East from Chicago to eventually end up in New York. But what if someone played a trick on you and gave you a fake map? Now, instead of an accurate map, you're working from an inaccurate reference point. You start out on your journey certain that you are headed East. Without realizing it, you get turned around and now you are actually headed West in the direction of San Francisco. Your only clue is the lack of signs indicating the remaining miles to New York. Your instincts tell you that something's up, but there's no reason to question the accuracy of your map. At any time, you could turn around and go the other way, but you ignore your instincts and keep following the map. If anyone else in the car questions what's going on, you staunchly defend your route. You can't possibly be wrong—until you finally become curious enough to stop and ask directions and someone declares, "Good Grief! New York! Hell no! You're headed towards San Francisco!" You are stunned, flabbergasted, and embarrassed because all this time you sincerely believed you were on your way to New York.

Okay. Now, let's go back to grief. The spectrum of emotions and sensations that come and go with grief are unique to each individual, nonlinear, and unpredictable as to their intensity and duration. It's quite likely that we might confuse one sensation for another, especially if we are dealing with multiple losses within a short period of time. The human being's ability to cope with loss and trauma has its limits. There is a point at which certain behaviors and responses kick in to assure survival and a sense of safety and well-being. I also assert that another factor at play here is our past and our comfort and familiarity with certain emotions.

For me, this phenomenon began with sadness. With the unleashing of many years of grief when I began therapy, Al-Anon, and Alcoholics Anonymous, it didn't take long for me to get comfortable with sadness. I practically lived and breathed this emotion. It was there when I woke up in the morning and when I went to bed at night. I have very little recollection of fun, joy, and laughter during this period of my life. Even with the new skills I was learning about grief, expressing feelings, and resolving issues from past relationships, I could not seem to move on. Any new loss only seemed to intensify what I was certain was sadness.

The turning point—or universal kick in the pants—was a broken engagement with a man I was about to marry. I lamented my sadness to friends and family for a lengthy period of time and then an older sister very innocently commented, "Maybe there's some mischief with your grief." I was insulted and appalled that she would even think that and quick to defend myself. How dare she not respect my grief process! I ended our conversation upset, indignant, and somewhat rattled.

At the time, a friend was going through rough times with her mom who had Alzheimer's disease and could no longer live at home with my friend. It was time to move her to a facility where she would receive the level of care and attention she needed. My friend was beside herself with grief. She talked about the depth of her sadness and how it seemed to dominate and color everything in her life. One weekend, we connected and she shared with me about a discovery that she'd made after getting curious about her sadness: what she had thought was sadness was not in fact sadness, but instead self-pity!

I found myself listening with immense intrigue. In fact it didn't take long for the bell to go off. That was me she was talking about. That was it! It was suddenly crystal clear that what I'd been calling sadness for years was, in fact, self-pity. I could never have admitted that to anyone because that would mean there was something horribly wrong with me. I had spent most of my life hiding that thought from everyone, so to admit self-pity would have been devastating. If people knew that there was something wrong with me, they would leave and then I would be alone. If that happened, I might actually die. That was my train of thought—quite creative and dramatic but not particularly grounded in reality. However, for me, those thoughts seemed real and occurred to me like the truth.

Given my fear of being found out and abandoned, it made complete sense that I might use sadness to mask the self-pity. After all, people could handle sadness and they might even feel empathy or sympathy. At the very least they would stick around and as long as someone was around I was okay. I would survive.

Can you start to hear the mischief? I have no clue as to when I crossed over the line from indulging my sadness to indulging in self-pity. The choice to live from one context to another was subtle and most likely unconscious. From that point on I spent an enormous amount of time and energy keeping up the masquerade. They were exhausting, painful, depressing years filled with self-induced suffering—maybe not consciously, but nonetheless self-induced. It's interesting to note that at this point in my life with all the therapy and my lengthy involvement with Al-Anon and Alcoholics Anonymous, I would have called myself someone who was fairly conscious. That is the power of mischief.

Could I have woken up to this masquerade any sooner than I did? I don't know. Was my life at that time any less sacred than it is today? Absolutely not. I can say that with certainty and passion today, but back then that thought was completely out of my realm of knowledge, wisdom, or insight. Had my sister not been curious about it, I might not have gotten riled up enough to pay attention to what she said, and instead continued to let the mischief play itself out for longer than I care to imagine.

Now, let's consider what this kind of scenario might look like coming from a sacred context.

My life again but fast forward six years. I am grieving my father's death and watching myself move through the process with keen interest and curiosity. The experience so far has been fascinating, extraordinary, and profound. Not without pain, but also not without joy.

Eighteen months into the process I hit a wall. I enter a two-week period of what starts to look and feel like apathy and depression. I'm not sleeping well and although I go to bed early, I wake up feeling exhausted. No matter how quiet or busy my day has been my physical energy is at the same low level it was when my father died. I don't want to be with people. I just want to come home from work and hide. It's all I can do to take a walk after work, prepare and eat my dinner, watch a little television, and then drag myself to bed. I notice myself not caring about whether or not I make my bed or do the dishes, and the laundry takes several days to get done. I become concerned about the depression and apathy so I call and schedule an appointment with my therapist. I also make an appointment with my doctor and ask her to run some tests because I'm worried about the drastic drop in my physical energy. After the appointment, the nurse calls to tell me everything is fine; nothing showed up on the tests.

For a bit I get caught up in the worry and concern, and I forget that what I am experiencing is sacred. I start to doubt and question things. Why is this happening? It has been over a year since my dad died. I should be further along than this. Why am I so tired? Something must be wrong with me. It shouldn't feel like this again; it should only be like this in the beginning. My mind is getting a workout and having a heck of a time at my expense!

Finally, when I have my session with my therapist I am brought back to "now" and reminded that every moment is sacred. I describe the apathy I feel and my "I don't care" attitude. He asks some questions and then leads me through a conversation about the absence of any permission to be tired or not care. Nothing profound is discovered but I agree to rest, reflect, do some journaling, and allow myself to not care.

The next two days I surrender to the apathy and start to get curious. I notice how my body feels. My chest is tight; my upper back muscles are in spasm, and my chest hurts when I try to take a deep breath. On the second day, I drag myself to the computer and start writing. Along the way I remind myself that it's all sacred, and that I am committed to not creating unnecessary suffering. Yeah, right. Sure.

I start writing and soon it becomes clear that I have mixed up my current feeling of apathy and not caring about my life with the two rapes that occurred more than 20 years earlier. I find myself reflecting and writing about my decision to succumb to the rapes. With the first rape, the man threatened to harm me physically if I didn't have sex with him. I got scared, not only for myself, but for my four-year-old daughter who was asleep in another room. So I stopped resisting, gave up, and then the rape happened. By some miracle, he didn't harm me physically and left shortly afterwards. I don't remember a lot except that afterwards I felt ashamed for giving up. I stopped caring about myself and let the rape happen.

As I wrote I realized that my current apathy had somehow become the shame and humiliation at what was a choice to survive a long time ago. The instant I read through what I had written, I was stunned. "Hmmm." I thought to myself, "Interesting." and then I began to laugh. It was amusing to see how I had mixed up the "I surrender" of the rapes and ensuing judgments of the past with the "I'm tired" and "I don't care" of the present. After that I was still tired but that's all I was.

That's mischief. It is sly and unpredictable. It happens when least expected and can take us down some dark and painful tunnels when we are distracted from the practice of being curious, staying present, and declaring, "This is sacred. It's all sacred."

So, now, the thing to do here might be to ask ourselves just how awake we are to our lives. Are we willing to be curious about our everyday words, thoughts, and actions? Are we committed to ruminating in our heads about the "myths" that prove there's something wrong with us? Or are we committed to being awake and present, holding each moment as sacred? The choice we make has a tremendous impact on the quality of our lives and the suffering we add to what life already doles out. It's our choice, and we always have a choice.

Chapter 6
Authenticity:
To Be or Not to Be

It's hard enough in our everyday lives to be authentic—fully self-expressed in our thoughts, words, and emotions. For most human beings, the challenge to expose our authentic selves is enormous. Consciously take that challenge into the domain of grief and our first inclination might be to hide under the nearest rock. However, early discussions and ongoing research regarding the "tasks of grief" make it clear that our personal growth and development depends upon allowing grief its authentic expression and natural completion.

All human growth and development can be seen as influenced by various tasks. These are most obvious when observing child growth and development. There are certain developmental tasks that occur as a child grows. If the child does not complete a task on a particular level, then that child's adaptation is impaired when trying to complete higher level tasks. (Worden, 2002)

Likewise, mourning or grieving—the adaptation to loss—may be seen as involving the four basic tasks listed below. It's essential that one accomplish these tasks before mourning can be completed. Uncompleted grief tasks can impair future growth and development. Although the tasks do not necessarily follow a specific order, there is some ordering suggested. For example, you cannot handle the emotional impact of a loss until you first come to terms with the fact that the loss has happened. Since mourning is an ongoing process, the following tasks require effort, so we often speak of a person as doing "grief work". Grief work takes time and energy and the reward of such effort is healing and peace. However, it is possible for someone to accomplish some of these tasks and not others and hence have an incomplete bereavement, just as one might have incomplete healing from a wound. (Worden, 2002) The four tasks of grief (referenced here as they relate to a death) include:

1. Accept the reality of the loss.

2. Work through to the pain of the grief.

3. Adjust to an environment in which the deceased is missing.

4. Emotionally relocate the deceased and move on with life.

Some people are able to accomplish these tasks on their own. But in many cases, especially when they involve unusually painful circumstances (for example suicide, Sudden Infant Death Syndrome (SIDS), and AIDS-related deaths), an environment that supports completing these tasks may be helpful. Although, due to the intense pain that sometimes accompanies grief, we might hesitate to seek out and find such an environment.

Interestingly, most of us go to a doctor when we need medical advice or information. Likewise, we seek out financial advisors when needing assistance or information regarding investing or managing our money. We learn the language or distinctions of these worlds: mutual funds, risk tolerance, malignant, benign, etc. We allow someone who is skilled at or has some mastery of these environments to help us. We listen to them, answer their questions, discuss our desires and problems, and then choose which aspects of their advice we are going to accept and use.

It's really no different with grief. Many people use and benefit from grief-related resources or "masters". Bereavement counseling is offered by many trained therapists. Most churches, hospi-

tals, medical centers, and hospice centers offer
grief support groups to the public. These groups
provide a structure in which people can receive
information about the grief process, get feedback
about what they're going through, but most of
all, can be authentic and fully self-expressed
about their grief.

Our friends and family members are also resources, but sometimes they aren't available for
whatever reason. Many people who are dealing
with the stress of grief have full time jobs that
demand they function and produce results no
matter what's happening in their lives. Some
work places don't have human resources per-
sonnel that might lend a compassionate ear to
help set emotions aside and allow the employee
to function at work with minimal disruption.

We now must face two dilemmas. One is the
realization that our everyday world isn't necessarily equipped or designed to provide an environment in which to adequately express our
grief. The second dilemma is mustering up the
courage and willingness to seek out a place
where we can, in fact, be authentic about our
grief.

Finding myself faced with these dilemmas was
a significant turning point for me that occurred
just before the first anniversary of my father's
death. I was still crying almost daily when I
talked or thought about him. I had a couple of

his shirts that I wore and when one became stained I wouldn't even consider throwing it away. My immediate family all lives in different cities and our communication is somewhat infrequent, so I wasn't exchanging stories with them about our father. When it came time for my mother to sell our family home, I was unable to travel there to help prepare the house for resale due to work and financial constraints. Consequently, I didn't participate in the reminiscing that occurred that is so valuable and important to the grief process.

My siblings and mother also coped with their grief differently—a phenomena that frequently confronts families. Most of them didn't feel the need or urge to talk about him the way I did, or they worked through that process with their spouse or significant other. Many of my friends had not experienced the death of a parent so I struggled with feeling like I was burdening them or causing anxiety by talking about my feelings or crying in front of them. As the one-year anniversary neared, I was suffering tremendously and felt stuck.

As fate would have it, several people suggested I attend a grief support group. I paid attention to the coincidence of their suggestions and asked a chaplain friend about local groups. He gave me several names of agencies but I didn't call right away. Since I'd participated in 12-step groups for many years, I noticed with intrigue my resistance to call. I procrastinated for a week or so and then my pain and suffering got uncomfortable enough to motivate me to pick up the phone and dial. The third place I called was a local hospice center and I was immediately touched by the warmth and compassion of the person to whom I spoke. I'd volunteered at a hospice center in the Northwest and had been moved by that experience, so I decided to check out this group first.

I was extremely nervous the first time I went. I was feeling quite sad that night and afraid I would cry the whole time. I was also nervous about talking about my father's death with total strangers. I had come a long way in my spiritual journey as far as being vulnerable and open, but checking out this group was pushing me to my edge. I remember walking up to the building and being moved by my memory of the respect hospice centers have for death, the dying, and their loved ones. There was an energy I felt that instantly touched my heart. I took a deep breath, pushed the front door open, and walked into an experience that would alter my life in the same tender, sweet way as my father's death.

It was a medium-sized room filled with sofas and chairs arranged so that everyone faced each other. I was asked to sign in and make myself a name tag, which I did. Then I sat down amongst the other six or seven men and women and took another deep breath. A few minutes later the session began with the facilitator welcoming everyone, and going over group guidelines regarding anonymity and confidentiality. She requested we all agree to not give advice but instead to just listen to each other. The guidelines she described were similar to those in Alcoholics Anonymous and Al-Anon, so I quickly felt relieved and somewhat "at home."

The first time I introduced myself was the hardest. I told them my name and then my father's name, and then shared briefly about how he had died and why I was there. My heart ached and my throat was tight as I tried to hold back the tears. We went around the room and everyone who wanted to introduce themselves. I was impressed by the calm and peacefulness of a few people who indicated they had been coming there for longer than a year. I told myself that I'd probably only need go a few times before everything would be fine. Today I smile with amusement at that thought as it was almost a year later when I no longer felt the urge, desire, or need to continue attending.

The facilitator was sensitive, compassionate, and skilled at relating what was shared to some aspect of the grief process. It was comforting to be reminded that what we were going through was normal, and that many others felt the same

way. It was with this group that I moved through
the first anniversary of my father's death. It was
also this group that very willingly helped me de-
vour a German chocolate cake (his favorite) that I
had baked to acknowledge and celebrate his
birthday. The room and group quickly became a
safe place for everyone to be authentic and share
our fear, joy, sadness, anger, confusion, and all
the other emotions encountered on grief's roller
coaster ride.

I gained many precious gifts from my experience with this support group. I was inspired by
others and found the courage to move through
the natural unfolding of the tasks of grief. I was
also blessed to watch others go from confusion to
clarity and from chaos to peace. I was moved by
their willingness to express their humanity. All of
these people gave me the gift of 'being' with me,
just as I gave back to them as we touched in with
our pain and stayed true to the task of adapting
to life without our loved one.

During that time I experienced the freedom of
being authentic at an entirely new level. Frequently I arrived feeling sad and afraid I might
break down and cry. Sometimes I did and sometimes I didn't. Sometimes we all laughed at something someone shared, and sometimes we all
cried together. I always went home feeling relieved and lighter. The generous sharing of others
kept my own loss in perspective while teaching

me compassion and gratitude. It was one of the most profound and scared experiences of my life.

I can think of no other access to the peace and contentment of grief's healing than authenticity. I personally do not know of any other access to all the ways of being that I both desire and resist other than authenticity. We make up a million reasons why we aren't authentic, but the primary reason is one for which we resist being responsible. That reason is the simple fact that we are not authentic because we choose to be inauthentic.

Granted, there are times in our lives where we held back because we feared for our safety and well-being. I'm not discounting those times. Our sensations of fear and the need to protect ourselves were valid. Whatever we said or did in those moments was appropriate and perfectly logical for those situations. But frequently there are situations where we know that we are safe and we choose to not reveal what's going on for us. Instead we say that we're "fine" or some other way than how we actually are.

If, as this book suggests, we were consciously bringing a sacred context to our lives, it would follow that every emotion, feeling, and thought we move through would in fact be held as sacred. And if our thoughts and emotions are sacred, it doesn't make sense that we pretend they are something other than what they really are.

Have you ever noticed how easy it is to be around some people, and how difficult it is to be around others? My own personal experience is that the people I am most comfortable around are extremely comfortable with themselves. Even when challenged by a difficult situation they are comfortable with that. For a few of those people I suspect that their being comfortable with themselves comes naturally. However, I am inclined to believe that, for most people, being comfortable with themselves came after surrendering repeatedly to their thoughts, emotions, sensations, and experiences exactly as life doled them out. Over and over they gave up the pretense.

The only way I know to achieve that kind of comfort with myself and life comes after removing all the "stuff" that I use to distract me from being in the moment. The distractions are a mixture of memories of past experiences, opinions, and assessments of how I think things should or shouldn't be, including myself. The quality of authenticity I am referring results from taking time to go within, notice what's going on, and be curious enough to stay with what's there and let the experience reveal whatever there is to reveal.

I consider myself a fairly authentic person and I would venture to say that when people comment on how easy it is to be with me, they are experiencing my willingness to be as comfortable with myself when I am being angry or sad as when I am happy, relaxed, or confident. The willingness I just described is a practice or way of being I consciously choose to express as the result of having the context of my life be sacred.

I'm not saying that the road to being authentic and comfortable in my own skin has been easy or painless. It hasn't. It has been a long and sometimes immensely difficult journey and it's not done yet. But I'm interested in staying present to and celebrating my life, confident that I will be okay no matter what's happening. Perhaps you, too, are in that place, and what's new is that you have experienced a loss so profound that you cannot get yourself from point A to point B and transfer that level of comfort to a new experience and relationship with your grief.

Okay. Let's look at that. It's my experience and opinion that there comes a time in every human being's life when we start to trust life. Otherwise we are left to strategize, manipulate, and push our way through every experience. For me, the context of a life of what I just described is fear. It shows up in many forms and when at the peak of its existence had me overly cautious and vigilant about everyone and everything. Now, there is absolutely nothing wrong with trusting one's intuition when it comes to fear. In fact, there is no one but ourselves who knows what's happening for us.

However, when we find ourselves face-to-face with grief, it would be easy to succumb to having fear be the context to the ensuing process. Fear of the pain, sadness, guilt, anger, depression, and the uncertainty of living without whomever or whatever it is that we lost. There is nothing familiar or predictable about dealing with the death of a stillborn child, a child lost to a drug addiction, a healthy husband suddenly ravaged by cancer, or the ending of a marriage no matter how long or short. These are just a few of the big ones. Sometimes the losses occur far apart and sometimes within a brief period of time. Either way, they challenge our humanity as well as our spirits.

Trust life when it looks like what I just described? Why not? It's the same life you trust to bring you joy and fulfillment. Why not trust that you can move through every single curveball it throws you? It's just life; it comes and goes. It doesn't let us down or give us more than we can handle. It might seem that way, but only because we think or say that. It gives us what it gives us and we have the opportunity, over and over again, to trust what has been given, step out into the unfamiliar, and be completely authentic.

The experience of trust that I'm talking about here is a lot like jumping out of an airplane. You have no clue as to what you're going to think or feel on the way down or as you take that first brave step into the vast space just outside the plane. But you take that step anyway and it's simultaneously exhilarating and terrifying. Thousands of people do that all the time. We even have a word for it. It's called skydiving!

I'm being facetious here, but when we take a hard look at our lives, we'll see that there are many situations in which we consciously step into freefall. Perhaps we think it's more okay when we do the choosing ourselves and can predict and control our emotions. Unfortunately, life isn't that accommodating or convenient. My intention here is not to frighten you. My intention is to wake you up and in that awakening your heart just might open. And in that opening you enter the sacred space of your grief and healing, a space of trust, peace, and authenticity.

I have tremendous compassion for what it takes to fully embrace the pain and sadness of one's grief. I am also completely confident that you are up to that challenge and have everything within yourself that it will take to get through it. Even if your most recent loss has uncapped earlier years of unexpressed or unresolved grief.

It all starts with a leap of faith into freefall...

Chapter 7
Uncertainty:
Hanging-Out in Freefall

With every ending there is the space for what's next. This is the natural order of life moment to moment, lifetime to lifetime. Something ends—a job, career, friendship, or a life—and immediately there is an opening for something new. Every ending offers us the chance to step into freefall, that vast space of infinite possibility, present moment awareness, and, of course, complete and utter uncertainty.

Most human beings are not particularly conscious of the natural unfolding of life. We might be distracted by our resistance to what's happening or by our fear of the ending or beginning, or we are caught up in the intense pain brought on by the loss. We don't pause long enough to watch for what's beginning to unfold. At the core of our resistance is that human pull to control what's happening and figure out how to be anywhere but where we are right now. Especially when right now involves pain. For most of us, to consciously step into the uncertainty and freefall that comes with grief would be absolute insanity.

Having life be predictable seems to be so much more comfortable, and to some degree it is. There are many times when predictability is exactly what we need in order to move through our healing. In these situations our intuition and feedback from family, friends, and professionals encourage us to rest in a quiet, comfortable space. However, there are also many times when it's clear that life is taking us in a new direction, that there is complete safety, and we consciously do everything in our power to avoid experiencing the uncertainty of what's next.

When life is comfortable and predictable, we can eventually become either bored by the lack of spontaneity or overwhelmed by the drama and suffering that is a by-product of our assessment of what's happening. Our belief that strategizing and predicting our way through life is always in our best interest is an illusion. Consequently, our efforts to control our destinies often end up producing discontentment and suffering rather than comfort. There can be no comfort because we always want to be some place other than where we are.

New beginnings dwell in the domain of the unknown and uncertain. This is not where most human beings want to hang out. Even if we are enlightened enough to want to be there, there is often a high degree of anxiety and resistance to being with or embracing the tension of these uncertain moments. Given all of that, let's take a look at how this applies to our losses and the grief process.

The whole of mankind is both enraptured and bewildered by the mystery of life. We find ourselves pondering certain questions at various points in our lives. As we grow older we start to wonder, "Who am I?" or "What is my purpose in life?" and "Does my life matter?" If we are on a spiritual path, the inquiry goes deeper as we explore our souls, spirits, and the mysterious forces and energy of the universe. For some people, near–death experiences, transitions between life and death, universal energetic connections, and communication from the "other side" are common topics of discussion. For others these discussions are not part of our daily lives. When life is in high gear many people don't stop to ask "I wonder what our relationship will be like when (so-and-so) dies."

So, when someone who has played a significant role in your life dies, we shift into the bewildered state of this unexpected inquiry. If we are holding the entire grief process as sacred and allowing things to unfold, one would eventually consider how to create a new relationship to whomever it was that died. At that point in time, a space opens up to limitless possibilities and discoveries. Curiosity and intrigue would be present, even in the face of sadness and pain. If we believe that we are all connected and that death doesn't remove that connection, we would naturally ask ourselves, "What's next?"

We could easily take ourselves out of this sacred moment by resisting the confusion and pain that arise out of such a conscious inquiry. There might be frustration at not knowing how to create a relationship with someone's spirit, or even fear or embarrassment at doing that. The frustration and fear would be valid reasons in our minds to pull back or numb out with some form of distraction. Not only is this kind of inquiry unfamiliar and uncertain, there are all kinds of emotions that might come up. It's challenging enough to consciously create relationships when two people are alive. To do so when one of them is dead, you might think, "Ridiculous!" or "I don't think so!"

This is when pausing and remembering, "Oh, yeah, I declared it all sacred." would be useful. From that context you could create from the space left by the ending of what was once familiar and be with the uncertainty with confidence, excitement and joy—even in the midst of sadness. Remember, the sadness comes and goes. It's fluid, just like you. So both during and in-between the sadness and emotions there are spaces from which anything can arise.

Ever since my father died in 2004, I have both grappled and experimented with creating a new relationship with him. Since we cannot talk, hug, laugh together, have phone calls, or see each other, I have frequently thought, "Now what?" There hasn't necessarily been a need to keep him or his memory alive, but the desire and intrigue around a new relationship has been more like a natural part of the grief process. Sort of like, "Okay, let's see what happens."

For quite some time after he died I couldn't even bring myself to talk to him. Even now, three years later, that simple action can move me to tears, but since I declared my grief process to be sacred, I don't push it. Instead I just let it be and stay curious and open. It hurts a lot to realize that I will never hear his voice, feel the softness of his cheek as I place a kiss on it, or take his arm as we walk together around the local shopping center where he used to get his exercise.

Remember that tug on the heart I mentioned earlier? This is one of those times. The heart muscle wants to open and there is pain—a heartache. My initial response is to pull back and shut down to the pain but then I remember and once again tell myself, "Sacred. It's all sacred. Be friendly." I surrender to the sensation and eventually the pain passes.

For awhile, I would be driving or be alone in the elevator at work and reach out my hand and ask "Dad, where are you? I don't know how to find you. I think you're there, but I can't find you." And then, one day, I got it. He's everywhere; in me and around me. He's in every living creature—every flower, child, man, woman, tree, and cloud.

That realization began at a church gathering. We were having a farewell party for a woman who was moving away. Her gift to us was a journey through a walking meditation. As we began the meditation, we sat quietly and then she had us stand up and move slowly across the room. We became two lines of people walking towards each other as she described biblical places and invited us to silently acknowledge one another as our Christ-like brothers and sisters. As we looked into each other's eyes, I felt my heart fill with a deep and profound love.

I took a seat after crossing the room and then it happened. I experienced my father's spirit inside of me. In my heart, mind, and soul—my entire being. There was a tingly sensation that completely engulfed and washed over me and penetrated every cell of my body. I had never experienced anything like that before, but I knew it was my dad. I began to weep and was challenged to keep my heart open to the profound love that I felt.

Did I imagine this? Maybe. Was it real? Maybe. It doesn't matter because it's part of the mystery and discovery of a new relationship with my father and it's all sacred. After I let myself be with and move through that experience, I felt compelled to call my therapist and get support in creating a new relationship to my dad. He asked me how I wanted that to look and I was completely baffled. I paused and waited for him to tell me the "right" answer to his question. I wanted him to give me the quick answer rather than be in the openness of the moment and uncertainty of what to feel, say, or do. Having someone give me the answer can be so much more comfortable than grappling with it myself. There is something to hold onto, some ground to stand on when there's certainty or direction to where I'm going. But having someone give me the answer is not creation. Rather it's a way to avoid responsibility for my life and deny my ability and birthright to create my heart's desire.

Thus began a new experience of the mystery of life that is a natural part of the grief process. If I had resisted or pushed my way through the process, I might have completely missed out on this extraordinary experience. To this day I am still letting a new relationship with my father un-fold moment by moment. There is a slight tendency to be impatient and become frustrated at my confusion and the unknown. That's just me wanting to have something solid to hold onto that has me feel safe, but in this case there's nothing to be afraid of or to be safe from. This is my life and it's sacred. Have the tugs on my heart gone away? Absolutely not. They still come and go, I suspect they always will, and it's all sacred.

There hasn't been much anger directed at my father as I've grieved his death. I don't think I was particularly angry that he died. He was 85 and we had a good number of years in which to be close. Although his death came upon our family fairly quickly, we weren't necessarily thrown by it. When it came to being angry, I grappled most with being single and the fact that I was now left to deal with my pain and grief alone.

I have been single for almost 17 years now and always lived at least 2,500 miles from our hometown. There have been a few serious relationships during that time and some brief periods of dating. Mostly there have been long periods of working with the reality of being single and using that time to go within and discover more about myself. However, all five of my siblings are married so, from my perspective, they all have someone with whom to process their grief. Most of them also live close to the town where he died, can visit his gravesite, and were there as my mother prepared our family home to be sold. They have had the opportunity to inter-act at family gatherings and share stories and memories with each other about our dad.

My experience has been completely different. Because of the distance, I have made only a few trips home and had limited interactions with eve-ryone about my father's death. I call my mom weekly and a brother and older sister from time to time. However, we don't necessarily talk about my father. So, there wasn't anyone with whom to process my pain and thoughts when I came home each day to my apartment, especially for the first year when I was in deep grief. For a while I called my friends and eventually attended a grief support group, but it wasn't the same as having a partner comfort, hold, and listen to me.

I missed my father terribly and seemed to be having a more difficult time than my siblings. In retrospect, I suspect that as a teenager I did not separate myself from him in the natural way daughters do, so the bond between us was quite strong even though we rarely saw each other. I'm not sure why it was like that. Perhaps all the losses I experienced so early in my youth delayed that natural separation. Whatever the reason, I am absolutely certain that the dynamic between us had an impact on my marriages and the three divorces I eventually went through. Along with this, I rarely dated between my third divorce and a later engagement. Several years went by after that until the next serious relationship, and again a few years of not dating between then and my father's death. Consequently, there was a male energy missing for me. That really is an understatement. It was more like I hungered for it.

My father eventually became a main source for getting my needs met for male energy. I also leaned heavily on my older brother for the same reason, so it's no surprise that I hadn't dated much in a long time. It was much easier to lay low and hide when I had the safety and comfort of a father and brother. After time, it just became more comfortable to connect with them, so I never pushed dating. I didn't have to risk anything with someone close and could pretend that I was satisfied with things as they were.

But I'm in this freefall, right? So I'm watching and observing because that's what there is to do when one is in freefall, and somewhere in the midst of this space I get clear about the being single issue. Soon afterwards, I called my brother, shared what I had discovered, and promised not to do that any more. I told him that any interactions I had with him from that point forward would have no agenda. They would be purely sister to brother or friend to friend, rather than me trying to get an occasional "hit" of male energy or avoid dealing with being alone. My father and brother were now both out of the picture and I was left to grieve my father's death as a capable, adult woman in a way that had a truer sense of integrity to it.

So it now appears that I am once again challenged to step into freefall and enter the unknown as I create and define a new relationship with my father void of a connection to him that, although familiar and comforting, no longer serves either of us. That's the ending part that has moments of sadness, frustration, and bewilderment. But there is also a new beginning colored with excitement, joy, and satisfaction. For the first time in a long time I sense an inner shift as something new is unfolding apart from my former relationship with my father. It is a shift that I'm certain will impact my future relationships with men. Perhaps the connection is both ending and transforming. My father is now evolving into more of an observer than an active participant in my life and I'm experiencing a new and unexpected aspect of my adulthood. There is a sense of confidence and clarity that I could not have imagined would come out of delving into the mystery of "What's next" or taking a leap of faith into the freefall of my grief.

Chapter 8
The Middle Way:
Having It All

We have spent the last few chapters discussing the pitfalls of our preferences, the suppression and indulgence of grief, and our resistance to life's natural, moment-to-moment uncertainty.

Given all of that, now is the perfect time to discuss the middle way: consciously choosing to have it all—the pain and joy, the ups and downs, and everything else that grief offers. We actually began this discussion back in Chapter 4 when we explored how language and our preferences distract us from being in the moment. In this chapter, I want to talk about one specific preference: not to have grief in our lives. Ever. This simple, yet desperate act ends up eliminating profound moments that shape our lives as significantly as the moments that have us feel good or happy. Except that if we are honest with ourselves, it isn't necessarily fulfilling to pick and choose one emotion over another. In fact, being fulfilled is the last thing that comes out of the choice to eliminate grief from our lives. The task to discern happy (or good) from sad (or bad) is actually exhausting. It requires a tremendous amount of energy and vigilance, and rather than be fulfilled, we get caught up in an endless cycle of assessing, grasping, rejecting, and ultimately all the suffering we discussed in earlier chapters.

Over time, our resistance to grief's natural, recurring visits becomes a formidable obstacle to cultivating a friendly relationship with its natural process. We don't like it because it's painful and doesn't feel good. We have moments when we actually wish it would end once and for all, never to return again. It's like running into someone we never liked in the first place. We force ourselves to be polite, bid a hasty farewell, and hope that we'll never see them again—and sometimes we don't. But with grief, the next thing we know, something happens and there it is again. At first we act like we're surprised and then we become annoyed. We brace ourselves as if our mothers were forcing us to swallow some horrible tasting cough syrup or eat liver. We fight it to the death. It doesn't matter how good it is for us. We're not giving in, no way!

But the grief is there, so we tolerate it and attempt to predict or question how long it will last so that we can just get on with the business of living and be happy again. No more pain or sadness. Just the good stuff, thank you very much. But the fact is that grief isn't that simple. There are many faces to grief: disappointment, regret, guilt, anger, helplessness, hopelessness, peace, love, intimacy, compassion, and joy. To deny any of those faces is to deny a part of your self. It doesn't work and ultimately has a profound impact on our lives. We are powerful human beings with the capacity to think, so we keep thinking that we know what's best for ourselves. But many unimaginable, life-altering moments are ignored, pushed away, and lost along with countless opportunities for intimacy, self-discovery, peace, healing, love, and forgiveness.

If you think about it, our resistance to pain and the many emotions associated with a loss of any kind is almost insane. Life itself, even death and dying, is nothing more than a series of beginnings and endings. A moment occurs and then it passes. An emotion comes, and then it goes. A thought arises, quickly followed by another. A marriage begins and then ends. A career comes to an end and we grapple with the unknown and life without the daily routine that not only fulfilled us but provided financial security. And perhaps the greatest injustice of all, someone births us, parents us, enters our lives as sibling, friend, or lover. We cherish and enjoy the gifts of their love and then they die. "It's not fair!" we think or say. "It shouldn't be this way. Life is supposed to feel good." Really? Who said so?

There is no guarantee, and never will be, that you won't ever feel the depth of heartache, guilt, anger, or total devastation brought on by the death of a loved one or the crumbling of a dream just as it is about to be fulfilled. The sooner we come to terms with that fact, the sooner we can make peace with our grief and, consequently, with our lives. And it is only when we make peace with our lives just as they are in every given moment that we can truly have it all.

It's almost as if we have to grow up and stop the temper tantrum about what we have or don't have. No matter how much we convince ourselves that we are in control of our lives and destiny, life does what it does. Its ebb and flow is not selective about who gets to experience pain and loss. I can assure you that no one out there is always happy. To think that we will ever get to that place is an illusion, and when we can at last own up to buying into that illusion, we can claim our birthright to every profound and precious moment life generously offers and then takes away.

What would have us give up those precious moments? What keeps us from having it all? Language, pure and simple. Opinions come out of language and if we had no opinion of what life is supposed to look like, we could actually be content with what was happening, no matter how it looked or felt: joy or pain; sadness or happiness; guilt or peace.

If grief is going to come and go and if it's here for the duration—and I assure you, it will and is—then we might as well get friendly with it. And if we get friendly with it, we might discover that our natural interaction with grief is not unlike every other relationship we hold precious. Think about it. The family and friends you care about and interact with on a regular basis are not with you every day. They come and go; work, play, home life, church, recreational activities, and so on. In fact, if everyone were to be with you every day it would be one very taxing and crowded life. Your home would be filled with large numbers of dinner guests, probably more than the needed number of tennis players on the court, standing room only at church, and your boss and coworkers would be at your workplace during the day and in your homes at night.

What I just described is completely absurd. But that's exactly how many of us relate to our grief: that it will be there every waking hour of our lives. We don't trust that it will come and go so rather than allow it to be when it is there, we do whatever we can to completely eradicate it from our lives. Imagine what life would be like if we related to our family and friends that way. If that were the case, there wouldn't be much left to enrich and contribute to our lives.

There are a couple of other factors at play here. First of all, there is the pain. Every human being has some level of emotional pain tolerance, so there are some losses that we deal with more easily than others. The deaths of the parakeets I mentioned in my story are an excellent example of what I'm taking about. Piece of cake; easy come, easy go. But as we live and let in life and love, our relationships and attachments expand and deepen. All of a sudden, the pain that follows the loss of one of those relationships also deepens. So we start to brace ourselves, we toughen up, and we up our level of pain tolerance. And then wham! Life throws us one of its unexpected curve balls and someone you loved more than life itself, someone you never thought you could live without, dies.

For a while you're in that fog that settles in right after the shock of learning that they are gone. Maybe you get busy and distracted with the funeral service and burial. You handle the details of the estate, maybe make a physical move from one home to another, or go through and remove clothing from a closet. Then, at some inevitable point in time, there is nothing more to do but be with the pain. This pain is your birthright. It is sacred and at times can be intense; it might have you feel like you can't breathe; your neck and chest tighten, and you are certain if you give in to this pain you will die.

At this point the knee-jerk reaction for us as human beings is to pull back, close down, protect ourselves, and push away or ignore the pain. We do this in all kinds of ways and whether we realize it or not, the resistance to be with the depth of our love for another is the seed for what quickly becomes an unfriendly, adversarial relationship to our grief. For just a brief moment we feel back in control and sane. But it's part of life's natural ebb and flow, so there isn't anything to control. Still we pull back, try to slow things down. There is nothing wrong with what we do. We're human. But we pay a tremendous price for that false sense of control: we miss out on experiencing the honoring and celebrating of a love that life so generously gave us and then took away.

It might not be conscious, but I suspect at some level we refuse to allow ourselves to touch into the depth of not just the love we gave, but also the love that was received. I know that for me those moments of intense pain usually occur when I am present to how much my father loved me. When I get quiet and let myself reflect on his commitment to his marriage, our family, and his willingness to go through the challenges of parenting my siblings and myself, I am emotionally moved far beyond my imagination. I am taken to a place so unfamiliar that it can bring me to my knees, have me stop my car, pull over and weep, or in the early weeks and months after his death, fall weeping into a friend's arms. There is no escaping the love or pain. For me, the two become one and the intensity of that pain is almost too much to bear. When this happens, I surrender because I declared it all sacred and am committed to not missing out on a single of moment of experiencing my love for my father. The essence of this pain is love—that mystical human heart-to-heart connection that cannot be explained—and in that moment the face of this love is deep and intense pain. There is no getting around it, and I wouldn't want it any other way. The deep pain that at first frightened me begins to soften, mold, and transform me into the next moment of my being. And just as my living relationships continue to teach and shape me, so does my relationship to my deceased father.

At this point you might think, "This woman is crazy. Not going there. No way." Well, okay. You choose your path and I'll choose mine. But I invite you to consider that you will not know, understand, or experience what I just described until you go through it yourself after declaring sacred as the context to your grief. Your skepticism is logical and perfect. In fact, not only is it perfect, it is also normal and might actually lead to the experience of love and grief I just described.

A second factor that impacts our desire to completely eliminate grief from our lives is the fear that if we surrender to its ongoing presence, it will overtake or consume us; and if it consumes us we will die. We relate to grief as having so much power that it will never let us go. In this case, the extreme end of the drama spectrum might be that it is there to punish us, make us feel bad, destroy us, and beat us down. So, when grief arrives we do everything possible to push it away.

Well, my friend, consider that grief is your life. It is as much a part of your life as the joy and laughter, the fun and romance, and the delightful surprises. Its essence wants only to contribute to you. The natural process of grief is actually designed to heal. If you are willing to dabble in the possibility of a conscious relationship to grief, you could even go so far as to say your grief is an expression of love. Its energy—whatever "face" or sensation it reveals—comes from your being and from the love you feel for the person or creature that no longer physically exists in your life.

To suppress or resist our grief is like cutting off a part of our body, soul, and spirit. Take it away and we have no access to expanding the depth of our capacity to love, cherish, and be with another human being. If we cannot embrace love, even when it reveals itself as intense pain, how will we expand our capacity to love? If we cannot embrace anger—even when it is blind rage against the drunk driver, cancer, or whatever is was that killed our loved one—how can we expand our capacity to fully express ourselves so that we can heal? And if we cannot embrace our guilt—even when it is the drunk driver's deep remorse and regret—how can we expand our capacity to forgive others or ourselves so that there might be completion and peace?

When you look at it that way, our life actually depends on grief as the catalyst for transforming one moment to the next. You might even call it a natural dance or partnership. Sorrow leads to joy, anger to peace, anxiety to confidence, confusion to clarity, guilt to forgiveness, and back again, over and over with each beginning and ending. Eternally, thankfully, the essence of these beginnings and endings is our life. When we recognize this, our relationship to grief transforms from the unwanted enemy to that of a dear friend who we cherish and respect all the days of our lives and who cherishes us as well.

Today as I write this chapter, it has been three years since my father died. The intense pain still comes and goes, and when it does I still surrender. I go through moments of bewilderment that such deep pain could arise after such a long period of time. Well, at least in my opinion... Oops, there's that pitfall! But even that moment of doubt and questioning the duration and intensity of my grief is sacred. It passes and I move on to the next sensation, which could be anything from annoyance at the traffic around me or delight at bantering with a stranger in the elevator at work.

In between dwelling on how things were or were not in the past and worrying about what something will look like in the future there is a gap—absolute nothingness, the space for pure love. If I'm willing to stop dwelling on what I used to have (my father's physical presence) and stop worrying about what our new relationship is going to be like, then I'm left in that gap and present to my love for him and his for me. The heartache that I experience in that moment is one that I sometimes equate with pain, but it's really love. What I experience is the relationship, the heart-to-heart connection, my presence and his. To not be with that sensation actually pushes away not only love but the experience of my life.

I'm 54 years old and for the first time in my life I am willing to have it all: the ups, downs, and ins and outs of my grief and life; the adventure with my father and the unfolding of our new relationship; the ever-deepening relationship with my mother which most days is easy, and in other moments infuriating; the unexpected magical shifts in relating to my siblings that occur when I respect the differences in how we grieve; the uncertainty of the areas of my life that are not on solid ground right now, but instead are going through transitions that have me intrigued, anxious, annoyed, sad, or whatever sensation arises. When I embrace, accept, and honor each and every moment in that mysterious gap of nothingness, I get to have it all. We all do.

Chapter 9
Compassion:
Unbridled Generosity

We do all this grief work and come out on the other side for what? Sure we want to get on with our lives, not get stuck in the victimhood of indulged grief, or the emptiness of suppressed grief. But does all that pain and the challenge of getting through sometimes years of grief really have a payoff? Yes. In spite of our skepticism there is an immensely valuable quality that we cultivate as we move through our own personal pain. That quality is compassion.

As I reflected on what to include is this chapter, I became extremely frustrated with the difficulty in clearly distinguishing the value and importance of compassion in our lives. I suspect that is because it's only been within the last five or so years that I learned a technique to consciously expand my capacity for compassion. In addition to moving through my own pain and grief, this practice involves inviting in and then letting out the sensation of pain during meditation. It's called Tonglen, a Tibetan Buddhist meditation technique designed to cultivate fearlessness and compassion, and to show us how to love unconditionally.

Sometimes I do the practice well and can see its benefits, but by no means am I a master in the art of cultivating compassion. However, if I were to wait until I became a master (whatever that is) before I wrote this book, we would be in trouble because I would be focused on figuring out how to become a master, rather than take the opportunity to respond to the world as it is at this moment.

So, in the words of many others before me, we have to start where we are. You and I—both of us perhaps fairly new to consciously cultivating compassion—are going to discuss compassion's importance in establishing a sacred context for our grief and ultimately for our lives.

When we are in our own pain, sadness, and grief, the one thing all human beings desire, whether we are willing to admit it or not, is to have someone share it with us. We don't want them to fix or change things; we just don't want to be alone.

Have you ever noticed that sometimes when you let someone know you are in pain, all you want them to do is be with you? You don't want advice, a pep talk, encouragement, or an exposé on what's happened to them that's similar. You just want to know that you're not alone with your pain for the simple reason that having someone there with you is comforting. It doesn't change anything about what you're experiencing, but sharing that moment lightens things up and helps you move through it.

At least that is the desire, but unfortunately that's not necessarily what happens. Instead, people scramble to find words to fill the space. They say and do things that are well intended, although sometimes not appreciated, and it's almost as if their words or actions create distance rather than comfort. Any response to what you shared becomes annoying because in this moment when what you want most is to feel connected, you don't. Maybe the other person avoids making eye contact. They might shuffle their feet or pull their ear, or cross their arms. They might change the subject or end the time together and physically leave.

This kind of behavior is an interesting phenomena to observe, and I assert that we have all done this at one time or another—bailed out when someone needed us to stay. I also suspect that most of us have been on the receiving end of someone who just cannot be with our pain. On a good day, observing someone in that place can almost be entertaining. At its worse, we may feel angry, annoyed, rejected, or not heard. And in the midst of one of our deepest needs for human heart-to-heart connection, we are left feeling empty and disconnected. Something gets in the way.

Our natural state as whole and complete beings would not have this be an issue. There would be no concern to fix or change things for the person in pain or to pull back. There would just be a natural desire to stay close. If in fact we are already united as one being, as many believe, then it would follow that your pain is my pain, is the world's pain and that there is no separation of one from the other. If that's the case, it would also follow that being with another's pain would be no big deal. But, alas, once again, we are human beings who have language and those two simple facts have us inevitably make it a big deal.

Someone shares their pain; they cry, weep, sob, express anger, self-pity, or hopelessness— whatever is the source of their pain in that moment—and our immediate response is to pull back and protect ourselves. It is challenging enough to be with our own pain. Why on earth would we want to be with someone else's?

Because it makes a difference for the other person and for ourselves. They are comforted by our presence and we get to experience an open heart; and in the opening of our hearts, we let in another piece of the world.

Warning: If you are interested in keeping the world at arm's length and spending most of your life feeling safe, then you shouldn't bother reading the remainder of this book. There's nothing wrong with that. Just close it, put it down, and go on with your life until you no longer have the desire to allow your fear of people and the pain of life to keep the world at bay. If, however, you're interested in dismantling your self-imposed walls and opening up to rich, profound experiences with others, then keep reading.

I am not about to soft shoe this. There isn't time. Every day precious moments pass by when people we know and care about, including us, suffer unnecessarily. It doesn't have to be that way. In fact, I don't believe that life even intended for it to be that way. When we set aside all that distracts us from extending compassion to another—all the stuff of our daily lives and the advances in technology that reduce our human-to-human connections—there is space to once again enter our natural state of being, whole and complete with another as one.

The path to compassionate living involves getting outside ourselves and stepping into another's world. Sometimes I don't mind doing that because the other world is acceptable by whatever standard or opinion I have. If it occurs for me as safe, workable, controlled, and not chaotic, I am more willing to go there. However, when the situation doesn't match what I just described, I hesitate because it might take me into unfamiliar and uncharted territory. Situations like listening to someone as she describes an incident of domestic violence or sexual abuse. Or being with someone whose spouse, parent, or child was murdered. Or comforting someone who has just buried a stillborn baby.

These are not ordinary, everyday opportunities to get into someone else's world, but they happen. They are a part of life and sometimes happen to people we are close to, so there is a natural desire to extend comfort and be with them. But we get scared and hesitate, and in that moment of hesitation we have the opportunity to choose. We can move towards what scares us and trust that we have the capacity to be compassionate, even with someone whose situation is far beyond anything we could imagine, or we can pull back.

If we are committed to making a difference and being completely with and in the world, we will inevitably be invited to show compassion for situations which we ourselves have not experienced. If you think about it, relating to what someone shares when we have been through something similar is natural and easy. We know that we are not alone in what we have experienced and there is comfort in that. That very same desire for comfort and to share one's pain permeates the universe and the whole of mankind. To share another's pain is our birthright, even if we cannot relate to what they are experiencing, and a necessary part of the unfolding of humanity and community. When there are airplane disasters, or people who experience the violence and pain of war together, or hideous atrocities, a coming together occurs that allows each individual to move through their healing process. Not necessarily are their experiences and processes the same, but whether or not we realize it, the pull to be there for one another is as natural as breathing in and out.

Unfortunately, human beings are very clever at finding ways to distract themselves from being in their natural state with one another. It doesn't matter if we are sharing joy or pain, bliss or disappointment, or desire or disgust. If we were to put the same amount of energy into a practice that cultivates compassion as we put into the practices we have that separate us from each other, the world would occur for us as completely altered. That is because our relationship to the world would be completely altered—and the access to that level of alteration is compassion.

So now, this simple act of declaring our grief, and actually our entire lives, as sacred, becomes one of unbridled generosity. We now become willing to contribute to our loved ones, our neighbors and coworkers, our communities, our nations, and ultimately to the entire world. You might ask, "Am I interested in contributing to and having that kind of relationship to the world?"

The choice to live compassionately is inevitable. For every human being, at some crucial turning point, it can no longer be just about me. At that point, all there is to do is choose. Yet there are some obstacles to creating a sacred context that would keep us from expanding and strengthening our capacity to express compassion. The greatest obstacle is one that we have discussed in previous chapters: fear.

Now we're back to where we first began this book. Fear only exists through language. Without language fear is only a sensation, and even at that, it is only a sensation because we invented the word "sensation." In its purest form fear is nothing. It just is. However, for the sake of this discussion and what is probably a universal relationship to fear, I assert that if you were to explore that sensation at depth, you might discover that the sensation of fear is not easily discerned from the essence of many other emotions. Fear is nothing more than a form of energy experienced in one's body. No big deal, right? But it seems to have such power over us, so exactly what is the big deal?

Well, the big deal is of our own doing. As adults, the level to which we allow the sensation of fear and everything else we associate with that sensation to keep us from moving towards another human being and their pain is up to no one but ourselves. This is not necessarily true for those individuals who do not have complete and full use of their mental and emotional capacities. But if you're reading this book and grasping what I am talking about, then I assume you have complete use of those capacities. As such, I assume you have the ability to discern when fear is valid and to be heeded and when it is not.

I also assert that most of the time, when faced with the choice to be with someone and their pain or to emotionally or physically leave, the sensation of fear is not an intuitive alarm but rather a self-created guardian to one's heart, a safeguard against discomfort. That guardian ultimately becomes a barrier to protect us from the opening up and strengthening of the heart muscle that simultaneously accesses and cultivates compassion.

So what there is to do is dismantle all the barriers we set in place to protect us not just from the world, but from our own natural processes, including grief. The choice to allow our deepest, most profound moments of grief to remove our armor and bring down the barriers is an act of courage and generosity. The journey from that point forward is not only sacred, but a unique individual experience. You're the only one who knows how the barriers got there in the first place, and you're the only one who knows how to dismantle them.

At this point, the experience of our grief might present us with the sensation of being alone. What a paradox. To be with the world, one must experience oneself, by oneself. Not in the traditional sense of being alone, but in the sense of being the only one responsible for our lives, for the sacredness of our lives, and for the level to which we are willing to be part of a ripple affect that contributes to the healing and evolution of the entire planet.

Chapter 10
Making Waves:
Little Stone, Big Sea

The final and perhaps most important consideration in creating a sacred context to our grief is its impact on the entire planet. There is value in global thinking here, so for the sake of this discussion I invite you to step outside of yourself, beyond where you have stepped before. I also invite you to set aside your opinions or beliefs about how the world was created or how it functions as one and instead read this chapter from a neutral reference point—from nothing. You might say that I'm asking you to step into freefall, right here, right now, and in the vast space of this freefall we are going to explore making waves.

There are many, including myself and perhaps yourself, who believe that at some unseen, energetic level every creature and human being in the universe is connected. This connection is sometimes referred to as the collective consciousness and it operates at the physical, mental, and spiritual level—one cosmic mind and presence that sources and sustains everyone and everything. Whether it's individual or collective, that state of mind naturally affects change because change—the ebb and flow of life—is the essence of its being. And if change arises from and is the essence of conscious thought, it might behoove us to consider the impact of our thoughts, words, and actions on the collective consciousness—the ripple effect, so to speak, of a little stone tossed into a big sea.

Everything we have discussed so far has focused on having a sacred context to our grief and allowing ourselves to experience the ebb and flow of grief as an essential life process. The result of living from that context is a life lived fully, not held back by or stuck in unresolved grief. We live our lives completely and we claim and have it all—the ups and downs, and the opportunities we create from our passions, purpose, and desire to make a difference. However, if we are all part of the collective consciousness and if our thoughts, words, and actions are fueled by suppressed or unresolved grief, somewhere else on the planet there is an impact of whatever sensation or emotion in which we are caught up.

Now, that's an interesting supposition and certainly not something most human beings entertain or consider. Rather, we get lost in our individual worlds and are quite convinced that what we experience in life only affects us. So instead of compassionately moving outside of ourselves and towards others, we separate ourselves from that which our natural state of love would have us embrace—all of humanity. We do this because, just like with our grief, we have preferences for how our world is supposed to look—who should or should not be in our lives, and to whom we should or should not show compassion. We choose one person over another and separate ourselves from the great sea of humanity and all the magnificent experiences it offers.

By declaring the context for our grief as sacred, we allow the process to heal us and expand our capacity to embrace our humanity as well as our greatness. We can then push further out to embrace our global family; communities, regions, nations, the world, and last of all, the planet. When we claim our place in the world, we begin to experience both our individual and collective impact on the occurring world. Whether we realize it or not, consciously arriving at that realization is essential to the well-being and evolution of not only ourselves, but all of humanity as well.

To courageously and consciously declare that we will no longer live from unresolved pain and self-induced suffering associated with the sometimes profound beginnings and endings of our lives, would set into motion a global presence that reflects love, compassion, acceptance, forgiveness, and joy in being in the moment. Just like with our grief, we still have no guarantee that pain and suffering would be eradicated. Remember, to eradicate grief is to eliminate life-altering moments, so the goal then becomes to both individually and collectively embrace and have it all.

That simple act would cause an enormous and significant shift in the critical mass. There would be a coming together of thoughts, intentions, and desires that would be expressed as peace in the face of whatever is going on in the world. Given that, the impact of getting lost or caught up in unresolved grief is immeasurable and unimaginable. There would be an impact not just on our own lives and our most closely-held relationships, but on the lives of people we most likely will never meet, see, talk to, or know about.

Our resistance to the natural unfolding of our lives, including periods of grief, can cause many forces that continue to fuel the fire of humanity's suffering. Emotional, physical, and sexual abuse from suppressed anger, intimacy issues, deep and unresolved depression (that medications probably don't even have a chance to impact because the grief hasn't been addressed), physical and emotional illness, divorces, and lifelong guilt all prevent us from getting on with life and forgiving ourselves or others so that we might be at peace.

This is where the Little Stone, Big Sea phenomenon starts. Remember in my story where I talked about how I either suppressed or indulged my grief and the impact that had on my life? Well, the ripple effect was massive: three divorces, conflicts in parenting, a constant pretense and inner suffering that played a role in my drinking and alcoholism, multiple geographic moves, and financial struggles. It was a long, dark period of life spent lost in self-pity, insecurity, and a desperate longing to both live and die. On one hand I was ready for death and almost invited it during the peak years of my drinking. On the other hand, I desperately longed to live a fulfilling, purposeful, and peaceful life. Quite a quandary, and that's just the impact on me. Now, let's take a look at the ripple effect of my unfriendly relationship to grief on others.

Intimacy issues in my marriages created impenetrable walls and communication problems that never got resolved. I'm fairly certain that all three of my husbands experienced a high degree of frustration and perhaps sadness at my resistance to physical and emotional intimacy. Financial challenges in each marriage resulted in the loss of one home, no movement forward to save for retirement, and the experience of constantly digging myself out of what seemed like a bottom-

less financial hole. My suppressed anger, sadness, and other emotions associated with earlier
losses factored significantly in arguments, conflicts in decision-making, and the small amount
of joy and bliss experienced in these marriages.

The ripple effect on my daughter was also
tremendous. This was a source of deep regret
and sadness for me for many years and most
likely played a major role in the complication of
my grief as time went on. Shame and guilt associated with my failed marriages, the rapes, and a
long history of relationship struggles led to a vi-
cious cycle of drinking and alcoholic acting out.
Consequently, my ability to parent and be emotionally available during my daughter's early,
formative years of development was drastically
impaired.

The impact of multiple marriages and divorces
factored into her emotional "baggage" and left no
room for me to effectively support and deal with
her grief surrounding the comings and goings of
step-fathers. She acted out much of her grief in
conflicts at school, ran away from home once,
and eventually turned to drugs and alcohol until
her father and I intervened when she was 15.
Since neither my daughter nor I was coping with
grief, any situations associated with the natural
separation of mother and daughter was fueled
mostly by anger. For a long time, the only way we
knew how to separate from each other was with

an argument so we spent a fair amount of time and energy fighting. Since I also had not dealt with the impact of the rapes, both of which happened when she was asleep in another room, there was a sense of danger that she experienced but couldn't identify until after she began therapy later in life.

For my immediate family, particularly my parents, the impact of my unresolved grief was evidenced by infrequent, if not almost non-existent visits back home. For many years I discussed what was happening in my life with no one, so trust and intimacy were replaced with physical and emotional distance, caution, and a pretense that I was "fine." One of my greatest regrets was a five-year period when I did not see my parents. Not because I was angry with them, but because I was lost in the shame and guilt about how my life was going. I'm certain that my pattern of frequent geographic moves, multiple marriages and divorces, long history of job changes, and financial struggles gave my parents much concern and frustration. All of these events may have also caused them to grieve their unfulfilled dreams and hopes for my life.

Last of all, from the perspective of moving forward and living a full and purposeful life, I was completely stuck. I was lost in my self-pity and sadness, and almost paralyzed by a self-created belief, based on the past, that the world was a dangerous place. I didn't talk to anyone about my fears for many years, so any risks I took were calculated and controlled. It's one thing to consider the ramifications and consequences before taking a risk, but quite another to calculate each risk with the intent to prevent what happened in the past from happening again. The impact of this unconscious vigilance was the death of my inner self. There was very little joy or satisfaction in what I did as far as my work or career. There was no time spent reflecting on my talents or passions, like my writing, that I might use for the greater good. Those types of inquiries were completely off the radar. I was stuck, depressed, and resigned.

Can you see the ripple effect? What I went through is not necessarily a bad thing and as we discussed earlier, all of it, too, was sacred. However, the ripple affect of what I just described also resulted in a particular quality to my life. I experienced very little confidence or calm, especially during difficult times. What I mostly felt was doubt, caution, anger, a desperate need to control people and situations, and resignation that my life would never change.

Now, I believe that it is absolutely human to go through the kinds of emotions I just described, but to live with them practically around the clock for more than 25 years is carrying it a bit far. Being completely self-absorbed in my "stuff" kept me a victim and well distracted from claiming my value and purpose in life and from considering how I might make a difference in the world. By not dealing with all that had happened, I could just hide, lay low, and play it safe. It was like I went to sleep for a very long time and the consequence of this life-long nap was a powerful ripple effect that reached deep into the lives of many. What I described above also doesn't begin to take into account the impact of my thoughts, words, and actions on other parts on the planet.

But in every situation and circumstance in our lives and in the world, if we are willing to wake up and surrender, there is a space for peace—a peace that comes with accepting and working with things just the way they are. We can wait until we are well into our 40s and 50s, or even our 60s before we push ourselves far enough out there and claim some responsibility for the workability and non-workability of the world. We can fulfill on our purpose or we can remain confined to our own little corner of the world. We can have it all, on a global level, if we choose. In fact, if the world is going to fulfill its destiny, we must have it all and to have it all we must fulfill our own destinies.

If we are friendly with our grief and allow it to aid us in peacefully working with our lives, ex-actly as they are, we might be at peace about the world no matter how beautiful or ugly it looks.

We stay in the moment and take actions consistent with our hearts' desires for a world that works, a world that gives space for it all. If we collectively hold those kinds of thoughts and take actions consistent with that, anything is possible. But we have to give up our opinion about how the world is going to look 200 years from now or even just two years from now. We just don't know and we don't need to know. In fact, giving up any past reference point or hope about how things are supposed to look in the future allows us to dwell in the domain of endless possibility. Instead, if we collectively come back to the moment, move through what there is to move through and allow our lives to unfold, there would be harmony, and the natural global response to that would also be one of harmony.

The world is going to go the way the world is going to go. If we give it space to be just the way it is, we might actually get present to the depth of our own love, fear, sadness, or whatever is there in that moment. And just like with our grief, the sensations, and emotions associated with our response to how things occur in the world will come and go. They are flexible, and ebb and flow, because that is the nature and essence of life.

We also might consider giving up wanting, as it will only continue to give us the experience of wanting. Since we have language, we can use that language to powerfully declare our commitment to having a world that is completely present to itself as well, rather than declare only what we want. We may not get to experience such a profound experience, and I can guarantee you that it would indeed be just that. Imagine the global impact of millions of people who are completely present to their lives. Not judging or assessing, but just being. That kind of extraordinary experience has to begin within us. It won't show up out there any other way.

Ultimately, if we allow grief to become our ally or friend, we might actually experience the world as our friend. No matter how it looks. For that to happen, we have to give up our expectations and agendas. The true essence of world peace lies in being with things just the way they are. Achieving that will require compassion on the part of every human being to have a world that is willing to be with things exactly as they are for longer than a few fleeting seconds. Our existence therefore depends on compassion. So the question to ask is, "Am I willing to join forces with my grief so that the world can experience itself as all that it can be?" I invite you to answer with a compassionate and courageous "Yes!" and consciously be a little stone that makes waves in a big sea.

Appendix
Self Reflections:
A Study Guide

The following sets of questions are intended to be used in the context of a support group. It is suggested that you work with a therapist or in a group setting as you ponder these introspective questions. You might want to answer each question by journaling or speaking your thoughts to a partner. It is the author's intention and recommendation that you read the entire book to gain the value of all the concepts presented before exploring and answering the questions.

Chapter 1

1. What's my earliest memory of a significant death or loss? How did I react to it?

2. What was the message I gave myself, or
got from others about grief or about
showing my emotions?

3. What's my first reaction when a loss occurs? What thoughts go through my
mind?

4. Who are the people in my life who are
safe for me to reveal my feelings and emotions? What thoughts or fears have me
shy away from talking to people about my
grief and sadness?

Chapter 2

1. What myths, stories, or opinions do I
have about grief?

2. Which experiences and emotions do I
consider 'good' or positive?

3. Which experiences and emotions do I
consider 'bad' or negative?

4. How many different moods did I experience within the last 24 hours? Were
they mostly positive, negative or both?
How long did they last (approximately)?

5. What would my life be like if I didn't prefer one experience, sensation or emotion over another, but peacefully allowed myself to have them all? How would that affect the relationships in my life?

Chapter 3

1. What are the words I use to describe grief?

2. What situations or aspects of my experience of grief reflect those words?

3. How do set the stage for my experience of grief or for how I experience my life?

4. What areas in my life have a lot drama and suffering? In which areas are things peaceful?

5. What would it be like if the experience of grief became a real 'page-turner' that would have me stay curious and interested until the very end?

Chapter 4

1. Which aspects of the grief process do I habitually (automatically) categorize or label?

2. Why do I prefer pain over pleasure? Happiness over sadness? What's the 'right' amount of time pain should last?

3. What areas of my life do I suffer about? How much do I trust life?

4. What's my experience like when things are quiet in my head and I'm not thinking or doing anything?

5. What would life and my experience of grief be like if I trusted life more and suffered less?

Chapter 5

1. When it comes to grief, where does how I act or behave not match how I feel inside?

2. Where do I consciously choose to pretend I'm feeling something different that I am?

3. Are there any situations in which I feel stuck? What primary emotion(s) seems to color those situations or experiences?

4. Does my experience of grief (and my life) indicate some attachment or preference to all the noise in my head?

5. How would my experience of grief be different if I chose to spend less time thinking and instead spent more time observing and being curious about what's happening and how I'm feeling?

Chapter 6

1. When I hesitate to let someone know how I feel, what's the fear or concern that keeps me from being myself or "authentic"?

2. What opinions do I have about support groups? Have they worked for me in the past and if so, why? If not, why not?

3. Which areas of my life am I willing to ask for help? Which areas am I not willing or do I resist asking for help?

4. What would it be like to not care about what someone else thought of me if I just let my emotions go and cried, felt angry (or whatever emotion it is that I struggle with the most to express)?

5. Was there a time in my life when I took a "leap of faith"? What was that experience like for me?

Chapter 7

1. What are some of the ways I act when experiencing new and unfamiliar situations?

2. What do I say or do to control situations when they feel out of control?

3. What emotions come up for me when I'm out of my "comfort zone"?

4. Which memories of past losses might be worth taking a look at with curiosity to see if there is still something to be learned or gained from them?

5. In what ways has my life become predictable? How do those predictable areas affect my being satisfied and fulfilled?

Chapter 8

1. Which "faces" of my grief and life do I deny?

2. When was the last time I felt that life betrayed me or let me down? What happened, how did I react, and did I survive?

3. What would my life be like if I could let all the losses, beginnings and endings, just come and go?

4. What would it be like to shift from thinking of grief as a process, to thinking of it as an integral part of my life energy?

5. Am I willing to have it all? If not, what's keeping me from that experience?

Chapter 9

1. What does compassion mean to me?

2. What's my first reaction when I'm with someone who is expressing deep pain or grief (weeping, crying, being angry, etc.)?

3. What's it like for me to just be still and not say anything when I'm with someone who is in pain? What kinds of things do I automatically do?

4. Where does my worth come from? What has people value and appreciate me?

5. What barriers have I put in place to protect myself from the world? Which ones have I already brought down and how did I accomplish that? How can I translate that experience to opening up to my grief and expanding my capacity to be compassionate and just "be" with others?

6. What would it be like to no longer feel the need to protect myself from others and/or the world?

Chapter 10

1. What kind of ripple affect might I have had, up until now, on the people around me and the planet?

2. What dreams and passions have I put on hold or given up on pursuing?

3. What inspires me most when I see someone fulfilling on a dream or living a life that they are passionate about and clearly brings them satisfaction no matter how calm, chaotic, or challenging things are?

4. What abilities and talents am I not using or cultivating that, when used, might contribute to the quality of life for those around me – and for those I haven't even met?

5. What would the ripple affect be if I were to make the effort to accomplish something that I've always dreamed of doing but until now have let fear, circumstances, and a long list of reasons stop me from accomplishing?

Bibliography

Chodron, P. (1991). *The wisdom of no escape and the path of loving-kindness.* Boston, MA: Shambhala.

Chodron, P. (2004). *Start where you are. A guide to compassionate living.* Boston, MA: Shambhala.

Chodron, P. (1997). *When things fall apart. Heart advice for difficult times.* Boston, MA: Shambhala.

Chodron, P. (2002). *Comfortable with uncertainty. 108 teachings on cultivating fearlessness and compassion.* Boston, MA: Shambhala.

Chodron, P. (2001). *The places that scare you. A guide to fearlessness in difficult times.* Boston, MA: Shambhala.

Chodron, P. (2005). *No time to lose. A timely guide to the way of the bodhisattva.* Boston, MA: Shambhala.

Chopra, D. (2006). *Life after death. The burden of proof.* New York: Harmony.

Dass, R. (1985). *How can I help? Stories and reflections on service.* New York: Knopf.

Levine, S. (1979). *A gradual awakening.* New York: Anchor Books.

Levine, S. (1991). *Guided meditations. Explorations and healings.* New York: Anchor Books.

Levine, S. (1982). *Who dies? An investigation of conscious living and conscious dying.* New York: Anchor Books.

Lintermans, G. & Stoltzman, M. (2006). *The Healing Power of Grief: The Journey Through Loss to Life and Laughter.* Naperville, IL: Sourcebooks.

Moore, T. (1992). *Care of the soul. A guide for cultivating depth and sacredness in everyday life.* New York: Harper Collins.

Moore, T. (2004). *Dark nights of the soul. A guide to finding your way through life's ordeals.* New York: Harper Collins.

Myss, C. (1996). *Anatomy of the spirit. The seven stages of power and healing.* New York: Three Rivers Press.

Myss, C. (2001). *Sacred Contracts. Awakening your divine potential.* New York: Three Rivers Press.

Pitts, D. (2007). *Shadow living. Paintings of grief.* New York: Harobed House.

Rando, T. (1984). *Grief, dying, and death. Clinical interventions for caregivers.* Chicago, IL: Research Press.

Small, J. (2001). *Psyche's seeds: The 12 sacred principles of soul-based psychology.* New York: Tarcher.

Tolle, E. (1999). *The power of now. A guide to spiritual enlightenment.* New York: New World Library.

Trungpa, C. (1984). *Shambhala. The sacred path of the warrior.* Boston, MA: Shambhala.

Welshons, J.E. & Dyer, W. (2003). *Awakening from grief. Finding the way back to joy.* New York: New World Library.

Williamson, M. (2004). *The gift of change. Spiritual guidance for a radically new life.*

Worden, J. (2002). *Grief counseling and grief therapy. A handbook for the mental health practitioner.* Reproduced with the permission of Springer Publishing Company, LLC, New York, NY 10036.

About the Author

Leslee Tessmann was born and raised in the small rural community of Watertown, Wisconsin. Her parents kept busy raising their family of four daughters and two sons. Just after high school, Leslee moved to the Seattle, Washington area to attend school at Bellevue Community College. That move lasted 31 years, as she eventually married, gave birth to her daughter, and established a marketing consulting company.

Ever since her teenage years, bold, tight writing has come easily for Leslee. Over time, as she worked her way into the marketing arena, she honed those skills and enjoyed the rewards and satisfaction that followed. A 12-year career as a marketing consultant in the Northwest earned her a solid niche as a powerful, results-producing writer. Her deftness at blending technical material with eloquent, persuasive writing in well-organized documents saw her engineering and architectural clients reap the rewards through increased interviews and multi-million dollar signed contracts. Over time, she shifted out of the technical writing industry and began to focus her talent and energy on subjects about which she was passionate.

As her story in *Sacred Grief* describes, a series of challenging circumstances propelled her into a time of self-discovery. The recognition of her alcoholism and ensuing sobriety in 1994 pushed her into her first conscious experience with deep, unresolved grief. She became active in Al-Anon and Alcoholics Anonymous and eventually shared about her recovering at treatment centers, colleges, and Al-Anon and AA meetings and retreats. Her authentic, straight-forward expression of life before and after recovery was appreciated and acknowledged by her audiences. Over time she went on to create and facilitate classes that dealt with working with life on life's terms, a large part of what *Sacred Grief* is all about.

Leslee's move from Seattle to Houston in 2003 and her father's death in 2004 were the catalyst for surrendering to her unfolding grief with curiosity and compassion, and the telling of *Sacred Grief*. It is her first and perhaps most memorable achievement at writing and publishing a book about that which she is so passionate. To accomplish this out of a desire to help shift the Western world's relationship to grief and contribute to the natural unfolding of the planet is to have one of her most closely-held dreams come true.

Leslee currently lives in Houston, Texas, with her two brown tabby cats, Kayla and Max. She travels to Seattle as often as possible to visit her daughter, son-in-law, and three grandchildren. Leslee is currently facilitating workshops, lecturing, and developing a book of straight-from-the heart prayers for times of grief and a book that explores the complexities and dimensions of guilt.

Index

Printed in the United States
201560BV00003B/1-141/P

9 781932 690538